to Margaret Leiming.

with my Kindest Regards -

Ben Nicol   July 1993

The World, A Canvas

TRAVELS WITH AN ARTIST'S EYE

Misty St Paul's, oil on canvas, 36" × 48"

The World, A Canvas

TRAVELS WITH AN ARTIST'S EYE

ben maile

Quiller Press

DEDICATION — TO BARBARA

My wife, helpmate, inspiration and critic.

She saw every picture in this book when they were canvases, from their blank beginnings to final completion.

Some were only yesterday, some a long time ago, and there were many that never reached these pages at all.

But none would have been worth painting had she not been there.

First published 1985 by Quiller Press Ltd
50 Albemarle Street, London W1X 4BD

Copyright © 1985 Ben Maile
ISBN 0 907621 45 7

Designed by Tim McPhee
Production in association with Book Production Consultants, Cambridge
Printed in Italy (KEL)

Contents

Ben Maile - whom I have known for a number of years -
is a truly remarkable man.

He is an extremely talented painter - as is evidenced
by the wide range of industrial and other commissions
he has received during the course of his life.

The qualities, however, that have endeared him to so
many are his enormous enthusiasm and immense
generosity. To my certain knowledge - he has
devoted much of his time to helping a wide variety
of worthy causes.

I only hope you will enjoy reading his book as much
as I have.

Introduction

Artists, by the very nature of their profession, tend to be 'loners'. The image of difference, the mould of rebellion is so often part of their uniform and armour.

Though Ben Maile may be a loner and a decidedly individual character, he has not followed the normal artistic path of art for art's sake, but then he prefers to be called a 'PAINTER' and any rebelling he has done has been against what he terms the 'affectations' of the art world.

Ben's workmanlike application to his craft has carried him successfully through a career where he has spanned illustrated sign-writing, selling in the open air art shows of London, the swish galleries of Mayfair and the very businesslike big store galleries, such as the House of Fraser group, Selfridges, and Harrods. He was an instant success when the leading art print publishing houses were looking for new work in the late fifties and early sixties.

But several appearances in the 'Top Ten Artists of the Year' in the print world did not seduce him into the easy trap of staying with this format where its constant and heady exposure can blunt judgement as well as creative talent.

Selling direct to a very critical tourist public in the summer shows of London (a most leavening and invaluable experience he says) gave him the incentive to open up his own retail gallery in Cornwall. When the inevitable success of this venture developed into three substantial businesses, spread across the county, plus his own art publishing company, there came the moment when he had to choose between the exciting entreprenurial role and the more intensively creative but lonelier one of the painter. Fortunately for his collectors and his work he chose the latter.

Some totally unique industrial commissions have absorbed his talent in recent years, involving North Sea Oil Platforms, Alaska Pipeline, the Thames Flood Barrier, and, if it can be loosely put into such a class, the *Mary Rose* epic.

Ben Maile's wonderland, always a source for new painting material, has never abated and his sketch-book and acute visual senses have reaped a rich reward in travels that have taken him literally around the world.

This book gives the reader not only the painter's viewpoint but depicts how the same painter's vision and imagination recorded the many scenes and places he has visited.

Royston Davies

Reflections from Barbara. . .

Ben Maile the painter is a difficult person to write about and I say this as his wife of many years. Distrustful of flowery praise, he shies away from profound statements about his art, and can flatten an earnest enquiry regarding his painting with "I just paint pictures and people like them or they don't." This rather flip comment does not do him justice, and if you could take a peek inside the character of the man, you would find his dedication to his craft (rather than art) and also the strong core of professionalism. I think he would rather be called a professional than anything else. His devotion to research and his advice to young aspiring artists to "look, look and look again; see your subject with your eyes and with your mind before you put a pencil to paper", are the golden rules he lives by.

What is he like? He has a mercurial temperament, a great sense of humour, loves music, animals, and has sudden bouts of 'keep fit'. All these, me included, have to take a back seat when he is painting. There can be a tremendous burst of rage if he gets interrupted when working.

As Ben's wife, I am often asked if I paint as well. When I say "No" people seem surprised, but I cannot see why a wife should necessarily have the same career as her husband. I have the pleasure of going with Ben on most of his trips and you the reader hardly need telling that organizing the travel and smoothing Ben's path is a full-time but rewarding task. Remember too that I see places like Venice, Rome, the raising of the *Mary Rose,* first as an experience and then fruitfully through the eyes of Ben's paintings.

If you were to ask me what I have enjoyed most, I would have to say the trips concerning the *Mary Rose* and particularly the making of the documentary film *The Cornish Miner in America.* The plight of our forefathers, hard-working and tough, proud to be American but fiercely proud too of their Cornish heritage, made this a memorable and poignant visit.

I have recorded many of our travels over the years, happy that Ben prefers me to go on all his trips whenever possible, but chatty little details in my opinion are quite unnecessary in a book of this kind. It should be sufficient to turn to the illustrations of his work and see here the kind of man he is. His romanticism, the caring side of his nature, the humour is all there for everyone to see.

Barbara Maile

...and from Ben Maile

Painting is primarily a visual craft. That tenet has influenced my views for years. Fostered as well by the torrent of verbal dressage that seems to have become as much the informative media of the art world as the work itself. There is so much explanation that one wonders if the work itself has any message left to give. To my cynical mind it has seemed that so much 'modern' art has jumped onto the band wagon, knowing it is safe from truthful exposure, knowing indeed that like the naked emperor of old, no one will want to appear ignorant.

This sceptical suspicion kept me from ever talking intimately and freely about my own work to other than a very few close friends. The quality of ageing, though, is the mellowing and tolerance it brings, and while my views on the 'nonsense' of art have not changed, I do now accept that the viewer, the non-painter, may genuinely want to know what makes the painter tick. Why did he paint? What were his thoughts? Those of course are questions that asked of a professional can be multiplied a hundred fold.

In general, I count myself lucky to be a working painter. I don't seek for any messages to give mankind. I am a recorder of things I see, imagine and dream of. Between bouts of frustration, jubilation and despair I find great pleasure and sometimes total satisfaction in doing what I do. But no creative craftsman can live but briefly without sharing, visually, his product. The outside world has to see it – and, if only one person finds some emotional response to it, then that is the added bonus.

Perhaps the truest and most enduring facet of my professional life has been that I have always painted what I wanted to paint. If galleries or clients were crying out for my 'boats' then they got boat scenes that I was happy to paint. Could I produce a series of Paris Scenes? Could a duck swim? I love Paris. A walk through that lovely city with a sketch-book was a spiritual and mental feast.

Even my big 'industrial' commissions were only undertaken on the basis that if I liked the scene – if I could find something in it to whet my painter's appetite – then we had a deal. If not, the deal was off. If that seems arrogant, think of what the customer wants. When B.P. briefed me the first time for their Forties Field exercise, they wanted a true, but evocative record of something going on there, the immensity and drama of the whole thing, but from a personal angle. They had a totally accurate and informative record by camera, but they wanted something extra – something that was just a little beyond the camera lens. It would have been dishonest of me to have gone ahead and produced a pictorial record of the scene if I had not been able to establish some sort of emotional rapport with the atmosphere.

I always remember a well-known portrait painter, with whom I had been privileged to share an exhibition. Looking at my work he suddenly said with quite apparent sincerity, "Ben, I *do* envy you – you paint just what you want to paint." Against my strong, enthusiastic canvases his portraits and *tromp l'oeuil* still lifes shone out like beacons. This was the work of the dedicated traditionalist. He had encompassed in one painting more superb techniques than I could learn in a lifetime. His shadows were the subtlest, the highlights the most iridescent. When I looked at one of his portraits I waited for the eyes to blink, so incredibly real was the likeness.

At that time, when my work was still showing three figures in the catalogue, his was priced in thousands of guineas. Society debs were queueing for his commissions and if you picked any crowned head of Europe, the chances were that the official royal portrait would bear his signature. And here was this revered artist envying Ben Maile! As I got to know him better, I began to learn the depth and sincerity of his compliment. As a high priced society portrait-ist, he still had to 'render to Caesar'. For all of this superb artistry and technical skills his painting had to mirror the view that they had of themselves. Rarely could he freely paint exactly what *he* saw. Perhaps more than any other he made me realise how lucky I was.

My life, of course, is not just a daily round of work at the easel, it is the immense variety that creates the enjoyment and excitement. Discussions with publishers, checking proofs at printing works, submitting designs for pottery, arranging exhibition dates, work-ing before television cameras, drafting scripts, discussing commis-sions, lecturing and attending charity functions. I travel to meet a client and view a new gallery, research some new painting ideas, and most particularly, travel just to find some new subjects. One of the most enjoyable bonuses that painting has brought me is to be able to indulge my itchy feet. But if someone asks me "What does painting really mean to you – what is it all about?"

This is the answer, the real ultimate enjoyment of just painting, the physical pleasure of setting out a palette. The big white blank canvas going up on the easel waiting to be attacked. Squeezing out from the fat tubes the rich pigment of favourite colours. The very sensuous feeling of working that pigment onto and into the coarse receptive grain of the canvas. Applying the heavy impasto of dark tones over which I am going to overlay the lighter colours, and the subtle reflections. I feel the onset of excitement as I try to match on canvas that picture already there in my mind's eye. This is the true aesthetic feeling – the real theatre of painting.

Only when I am there, at the easel, with brush, hands and knife and the thick rich pigment, do I begin to experience the pure intimate feeling of creation. The day I can no longer find that feeling will be the day I stop painting.

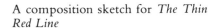
A composition sketch for *The Thin Red Line*

The Thin Red Line

Although I am constantly on record as condemning the verbal dressage and mystique that elaborates so much of my profession, I have to confess, however reluctantly, that one particular painting of mine originated in a dream. I awoke this most special morning with a vision so strikingly vivid it was reality. In my dream I had painted two large canvasses, both military subjects. Both very impressive. The visual impact of the dream was with me clearly for some moments of waking time.

The first of these 'dream paintings I completed in rough sketch with colour notes. The actual painting was finished within the next week or so. The memory of the second, however, faded while the first, *The Thin Red Line*, was being worked on.

What might be classed as a companion painting, *The Storming of the Hougoumont*, painted sometime later, at the request of my good friend Phil Needham, did carry out at least the barely remembered core of that dream. I had painted troops (circa Waterloo) storming a building. The colours, as with *The Thin Red Line,* were predominately blues and greys with overtones of red, but that first canvas was literally a 'dream' painting.

But to keep to my dogma of 'away with the mystical nonsense' – what after all are dreams? Sights, sounds and images registered upon the subconcious fed by imagination and reproduced when the mind is at its most receptive state, asleep. Certainly for many weeks previously I had been researching, reading and pictorially memorising page upon page of military history over the Waterloo and Crimean period.

The Thin Red Line aroused more than interest and admiration from Ben Maile collectors. Keen follower Tim Stonor added it to his collection before considerable publicity broke upon its introduction as a signed Limited Edition Print.

FROM TIM STONOR

Perhaps the most remarkable fact about Ben Maile's *The Thin Red Line* is that no artist has previously caught in oils this historic phrase.

W. H. Russell, *The Times* Crimean War Correspondent in a despatch to England wrote of 'the thin red streak'. It was on his return to the United Kingdom, after the end of the war, that he amended 'streak' to 'line', in his filed reports.

My introduction to what in my opinion and that of many others is Ben's best work to date was a 4″ × 2″ coloured post-card advertising the sale of 450 prints of *Thin Red Line*.

I had seen some of his work the previous year in his St. Ives studio and the post-card told me all that I wanted to know. A telephone call to Ben a quick conversation and the deal was done. *Thin Red Line* was mine. The decision to buy has never been regretted.

The picture has been a never-ending source of pleasure to my family and myself as well as to our many friends.

As a tail-piece let me add that my eldest son and my sister each have a print not to mention two of my oldest friends.

MR TIM STONOR

The Thin Red Line, oil on canvas, 36″ × 48″ (collection Mr Tim Stonor)

After all these years, it does no harm to mention that I became the target for some quite surprising and alarming correspondence. It was to my shame of course that in the initial creative enthusiasm I had totally forgotten that there was already in existence a splendid painting of the same title. In the Dewar (of Whisky fame) collection was a finely painted scene, by Robert Gibb, of this historic event, portraying, very realistically, the famous stand of infantry. The charging horses, clashing sabres and flailing bodies were all on canvas, a vivid representation of that Crimean epic. Mine bore no comparison. The painting I had dreamed up showed no charging cavalry. No actual clash of antagonists. I had shown only the frail but indomitable stand of British infantry. The fact that they were facing immediate assault was obvious.

There was a suggestion of collapsed figures, a haze of cordite smoke and the fine thin flash of bayonet steel, but actual combat, the killing, wounding and savagery were left to the imagination. A typical Ben Maile ploy on technique, some might say. So there were two totally different paintings of the same event, but I had used the same title. There is no copyright on title that I am aware of and the original title was corrupted from the historically famous journalist report of William Russell of *The Times*, who was there on the day and used the graphic description: ". . . A flash of steel above a thin red line."

I had to point this out gently to one irate critic, who wrote to me in furious tones, "How dare you Sir." For him Robert Gibb's painting constituted the one and only pictorial reproduction of that piece of history and I had no right to dare to emulate it, never mind using the same title. Having, as I naively thought, neatly extricated myself from that small embarrassment I was alarmed to receive yet another missive from my correspondent, which virtually involved me in a verbal duel upon historical facts. In retrospect it is an amusing, if slightly sad little episode.

Fortunately, my champion was the then C.O. of the Scots Guards, Sir Gregor McGregor of McGregor, and his very able regimenal adjutant. The opposition was a retired officer of the equally famous Argyle and Sutherland Highlanders. With such military might taking up cudgels, I retired, unhurt, unbloodied, and unloved but a little wiser in the matters of diplomacy.

The result of my dream went on to become a recognisably famous picture, but it nearly created the battle of *The Thin Red Line* all over again.

Crusaders

Long before I dreamed of *The Thin Red Line*, I painted *The Crusaders*. Its origins are now a little faint in my memory, but I know that having begun to carve albeit a small niche in the contemporary West Country art scene, with my Cornish harbours and fishing boat studies, I started to become restless, wanting new subjects.

My New York water fronts were one different aspect of treatment and my studies of London scenes, St. Paul's and such like,

The Crusaders, acrylic, 30″ × 48″
(collection Mr John Harvey)

were alternatives for both prospective customers and for the painter's catholic taste! But I was beginning to feel this niggling invitation. Do something different, something new.

Such figure drawings as I had done, up to then, were in the cartoon style, and I was wary of tackling anything of definitive portraiture. Nonetheless, in retrospect I recognise there was this deep-rooted desire to express humanity in the mass – on the move.

The Refugees, The Hordes of Ghengis Khan were still to come. I had painted the *Widows of Skopje* a year or two earlier, and felt I had almost to apologise for such a sombre, tragic canvas. I was, I suppose, still shying away from being thought of as an artist with a message! Perhaps there were still boyhood memories of *The White Company* or *The Talisman* whispering to me. However, I produced this large and effective painting some 4 feet by 2 feet and was then very pleased with the result; I still am. I look at it now, 20 years later, with an experienced critical eye and it still pleases me. We put it up, pride of place, in the window of our modest gallery, bearing the fattest price tag I had dared to put on any work then – 65 guineas! Resolutely (but inwardly quaking), I refused near offers, until the publishers, showing great daring, published it as a Fine Art Reproduction.

The impact of this painting relies largely upon the great expanse of neutral coloured background. Such colour as there is, portrayed most in the leading figures. I emphasised by the wide, light, surrounding space. The war train of figures disappearing into a grey misty distance is supported and given drama and romantic speculation by the space around them suggesting a vast infinity. One wonders what they left behind and what lies before them.

Influenced by technical requirements of paper size, machine capacity and, of course, costings, the publishing house decided, in their wisdom, that it would do little harm to 'crop' the surround, by an inch or so. There was so much space around the main subject matter, a little trimming would not impair its appeal. I had yet to become a regular winner in the yearly Top Ten Print Awards, and my objections were hesitant and easily, if politely, overruled. As a painting, it was generally admired and greatly coveted by many, as a print it was not a great success. The small but significant reduction of its supportive background had also reduced its impact. The scale of immensity had gone. The impression of a great, if primitive, army travelling over a vast plain was changed to a straggling line of individual warriors, leaving nowhere and hardly arriving anywhere.

Looking at that painting today (fortunately we kept the original in the family), it still retains its impact and drama, and were it to be published again – in its entirety – it would, I am sure, be an absolute success.

GUNSMOKE AT CRIMEA

Of War and Men

Undeniably, it was the pomp, glamour and ceremony of the military uniform and gatherings that first took my eye as a painter. When I began a little research, however, into military costume and history I was made more aware of the deeper drama and tragedy once more.

The Napoleonic and Crimean Wars gripped my interest and imagination, and whilst I attempted to portray the colour of uniforms, the dash of horses and the blazing of guns, I began to feel, inevitably, a deeper feeling for the humans as individuals.

Having started my military pursuits with Ghengis Khan and the Crusaders, progressing through 19th-century warfare, it is inevitable that my feelings and imagination should carry forward to the battlefields of my own father's time and indeed to the scenes of World War II where, like many of my generation, I was personally involved.

Though they might not appear in this book, paintings of the trenches of World War I and scenes from my own personal war are already simmering in this painter's mind of mine, and some day soon will have to be carried forward on to canvas.

The Storming of Hougoumont, oil on canvas, 30″ × 48″ (collection Mr Philip Needham)

FROM PHILIP NEEDHAM

Ben and I met more years ago than one cares to remember. The meeting was critical, my wife and I had kept tabs on the rising prices of the Maile canvasses over successive annual Cornish vacation visits. We were very well aware that these prices reflected the obvious and well earned success of the artist, in a way we were pleased that our own early recognition had been accurate and intuitive. On our previous years it had always been the same story: after the expense of a summer vacation should we, could we, also incur the additional expense of a Ben Maile original.

On meeting Ben we discussed our particular requirement for the projected canvas on a military theme. This private decision had originated from following Ben's digression into representational military works which had eventually crystalized into the stunning *The Thin Red Line,* a painting which captures all the apprehension and foreboding of that historical event on the slopes leading to the port of Balaclava.

We said please could we have something else from the Crimean era. Ben was very charming but the answer was a polite no. He ventured the explanation that his infrequent forays into British military history were of a purely personal nature and mirrored his own military interests and enthusiasms. The Crimea had been developed and at that point in time finished with.

When Ben politely declined our request the disappointment must have showed on the faces of my wife and myself. "Was there perhaps something else, another event and another place," asked Ben. My own amateur military history interests extended beyond the Crimea and I tentatively suggested Waterloo, a great field which I had explored on a hot day in late May a few years before. Ben momentarily considered the proposal and reacted with growing enthusiasm. The Crimea may have been finished with, but the Napoleonic saga was stirring in a plain café in Newquay midst red faced summer visitors in shirt sleeves and a sprinkling of local estate agent and office types in incongruous business suits. We talked a little more detail about Waterloo, and finally left Ben in Bank Street. On the walk back to the hotel, my wife and I felt as if we had blown the entire rent money on the favourite at Newmarket.

We waited many months for our painting – as I recollect, a serious, but passing illness and a foreign travel commitment all got in the way. The trip to the Dorchester Hotel for the exhibition eventually came and my wife and I met up with our painting on an easel in a prominent place in the exhibition room; it portrayed *The Storming of the Hougoumont.* Did this work really germinate from a meeting midst the rattle of cups and saucers in a bustling little holiday café in Newquay? It didn't seem possible. The classic *The Thin Red Line* is all dark brooding and solider's apprehension. *Hougoumont* contrasts with its energy, dash, and fire and captures precisely the nature of events at Waterloo on that day and at that critical place on Wellington's right flank.

MR PHILIP NEEDHAM.
Management Consultant.

17

ABOVE: *The Gun*, oil on canvas,
30″ × 48″

RIGHT: *A Time of Glory*, oil on canvas,
36″ × 48″

18

FROM NORMAN CRISP

One evening in the late 1960s, I walked into the cocktail bar of a Bayswater hotel. It was somewhere to dine, an idle choice, no more. An oil painting on the wall captured my attention, and I could not take my eyes from it.

Wherever the troop of cavalry were going, the riders had been a long time in the saddle; reins were slack; the horses' heads bowed. More real, more vivid than the glass and chromium of that cocktail bar was the stifling dust which plagued beast and man, the heat, the sore discomfort, the utter weariness of riders and animals alike. It seemed to me that I could hear the uneven sound of horses' hooves, the creak of leather, the jangle of harness, the harsh breathing from dust-clogged lungs. Looking at that painting, I knew that what the artist was telling me was the truth; I knew what it would have been like to be one of a troop of cavalry on the move.

Art, I knew little about, save a sketchy general knowledge from those youthful days when one is curious about everything, but I instinctively recognised that what I saw was good and true and something extraordinary. Along with the masterful and confident technique, there was pain in that painting too; whoever had done it had left a part of himself on the canvas. The barman told me that it was by Ben Maile. Enquiries led to a gallery from which I was sent some particulars. Presumably my name had been recorded because, a year or two later, I received an invitation to attend one of Ben Maile's functions at the Dorchester Hotel.

For the first time in my life, I acquired an original oil painting, *Trawlers at Sunset*. There can be love at first sight between man and picture too, and this was it. *Trawlers at Sunset* is a marvellous example of another facet of Ben Maile's work; no men here, but the artefacts of man against the majesty of nature in moving conjunction.

Meeting Ben Maile on that occasion, I felt as though I had known him for years, and not only because he is kind, outgoing, and has an eager, observant interest in his

fellow men. Perhaps we have a little in common, apart from both having served as R.A.F. air crew during World War II. Certainly I recognised that obsession with work for its own sake, which has nothing to do with the Protestant work ethic, but combines a hunger for creation which makes work a daily, necessary fix, and the pursuit of the next ideal with the recognition that any lifespan is limited and time is to be used to the full.

Ben's frank recognition of his own commercial worth, his practical and organising ability, his complete lack of *chi chi,* in short his sheer professionalism also made it singularly easy to respond to him. Ben Maile is a man who nurtures his given talent to the utmost.

Our respective worlds tend to

intersect only at intervals, but despite that, in the intervening years, as well as finding my walls further graced by his painting *Schooner in a Squall* and one of his delightful working drawings, I have also received the unexpected gift, not only of his hospitality for he is a good host par excellence, but of his friendship.

Just how this friendship emerged, occasional but ringing true nevertheless, is hard to analyse. Somehow, it was there, it happened. He is a stimulating companion, forthright in his views, yet a good listener, ever ready to consider differing opinions. Yet, for all his open manner there is, or so it seems to me, something unfathomable about him, a reserved, unpenetrated area never revealed to anyone save, perhaps, his close-knit family. Perhaps it is a veil for that private, secret vision he possesses, the gift which, with the aid of hand and eye, enables him to create for our benefit his own vibrant, living perception of the world we inhabit from mere paint and a dead canvas. Perhaps. I do not really know, and never shall.

What I do know is that I count myself fortunate that, a decade and a half ago, chance took me into that cocktail bar. Not only have I the pleasure of possessing examples of his work, but I met the artist whose paintings I so much admire, and found that I admired the man himself quite as much. It is one of my prouder boasts, to be counted among Ben Maile's many friends.

MR NORMAN CRISP
Author and Television Scriptwriter.
Playwrite.

Guns of War, oil on
canvas, 30″ × 40″ (a
Limited Edition orig-
inal in the collection of
Mr John Perkins)

Fishers in the Mist, oil on canvas,
24″ × 36″

Fishers in the Mist

When one has been ill it's always a relief to get back to normality again. That 'normality' for a painter means being able to paint again. My illness had been sudden and severe and a resumption of constructive painting eluded and frustrated me for some time.

Then quite suddenly everything clicked together and the painting shown here came to life on the easel. Dr. Brian Prout had resolved the doubts and misgiving surrounding my health and in turn became Brian Prout, fellow painter and good friend. One does not dedicate a painting – but if so, then obviously this would have been dedicated to a particular physician!

FROM BRIAN PROUT

My first acquaintance with Ben was a professional affair, when, as a consultant physician, I saw him with some troublesome symptoms. The consultations soon became a pleasure rather than a chore because he was always so full of fun and seemed to have such a wide range of interests in addition to art. We soon became friends.

I was very much attracted to his style of painting, especially as painting is one of my own hobbies. I knew that painting like that only came after many years of concentrated effort and trial and error superimposed on natural skill. Imagine my delight when, convalescing from an illness of my own, I was invited in Ben's usual generous manner to enter the inner sanctum of his studio and learn some of the secrets. The main lesson seemed to be how to paint 'loose' instead of 'tight'. How does an extrovert artist encourage an obsessional scientist to paint that way? Not an easy task, and many a time when Ben was not watching I would cast away the large brush and palette knife and pick up the drawing pen amd a small piece of paper in order to cartoon a situation in characteristic small obsessional style. Ben was usually at the receiving end of such cartoons and always took it in great heart with loud guffaws.

Notwithstanding the diversions I am very grateful to Ben for enabling me to produce several large canvasses on various subjects which are showing improvement and signs of Ben's influence so that a rather interesting combined style has emerged.

During the years I have witnessed Ben's paintings become increasingly exciting. It is clear that even an established and experienced painter continues to gain in strength with continuing long hours of concentration. No wonder his paintings are in demand, and I wish him well-deserved and continuing success.

MR B. J. PROUT
Consultant Physician,
M.R.C.S.(Eng), B.S., Ph.D., M.D.,
F.R.C.P.(Lond)

TRAVELS ON A
PAINTER'S PASSPORT

Passport to Painting

I have a love affair with a passport – mine, needless to say.

One might argue on the juxtaposition of a 'travelling painter' or a 'painting traveller'. Certainly one of those titles is very aptly applied to Ben Maile. Like many of my generation I always wanted to travel. It was not easy in the early days but when I was able to list 'professional painter' as the occupation on my passport, then my globe-trotting really started. A professional painter needs, from time to time, fresh stimuli, new ideas and visions. My love of travel, of seeing new places, meeting new people, became an accepted formula for my mode of painting.

Whether I board an aircraft or ship with a simple intention of arriving at a place I have not seen before, or if the visit is the result of a commission or desire to paint that particular destination, matters not. Inevitably my mind and my senses are taken into something new. It is a new experience and I relate to it as all painters do – I want to record it, for it excites me. It awakens that old enthusiasm once more and the need to transpose onto paper and canvas that which I see, hear and smell. It is more of an intuitive compulsion than an ordered exercise.

Thirty years ago, I could not have foreseen that my passport would take me to such diverse places as Alaska and Australia, Italy and North Africa, Germany and the U.S.A., Yugoslavia and Hong Kong. Each and every one had something totally different to offer. When I leaf through the pages of my passport it is like the nostalgia of thumbing through the family album.

Each border-post stamp or visa franking brings vividly to mind not only the place and the time, but the paintings they resulted in. So I love that little blue book, it turns back the memory pages of the past, and holds the promise of new painting in the exciting future.

Paris

Paris has always been the Englishman's idea of the Continent with a capital 'C', at its most exotic and uninhibited. For a painter, of course, it still lives under the influence of the Impressionists. Lautrec epitomises Montmartre (or is it the other way round?). Degas accompanies me to Longchamps and the elegant scenes of the Barres. I feel the presence of Renoir and Manet in the Tuilleries, and when I gaze at Notre Dame and some of the other singularly Gothic churches that abound in the city, I am mindful of that member of the group, Utrillo. His gloom and tragedy was at such variance with the wild gaiety of Paris in those exciting days.

Like its London counterpart Paris has its river, the Seine, which serves both as a living, moving lifestream to the metropolis and as a divisive barrier. The South Bank cocks a snook at the formal elegance of the city's centre to the north, whose citizens cross over the river to participate daringly in the vulgarity and *haute monde* that seems to be the trademark of the South Bank. But crossing the Seine they do so over one of those beautiful 18th-century bridges that were built with all that Gallic grace and elegance.

OPPOSITE: *The Pont Neuf*, Paris, oil on canvas, 30″ × 20″ (collection Mr Ted Coupland)

The Sacré Coeur, Paris,
oil on canvas, 24″ × 36″
(Artist's collection)

LEFT: *The Arc de Triomphe*, Paris, oil on canvas, 30″ × 20″

ABOVE: *The Place du Tertre*, Paris, oil on canvas, 28″ × 36″

It is strangely ironical that one of the greatest military despots of history was responsible for introducing that same grace and elegance into the centre of the city itself. From the Place d'Etoile (now known as the Place Charles de Gaulle), with its massive, imposing Arc de Triomphe and that incredibly long and spacious tree-lined avenue, the Champs Elysées, with its gardens and palaces, to the equally monumental Place de la Concorde; we may, in the middle of all that modern grandeur, forget that this remodelling of an old capital was the brain-child of Napoleon Bonaparte.

The very immensity of its Patrician splendour would surely have

PLACE DU TERTRE – PARIS

*However much some of the more
sophisticated may today dismiss the Place
du Tertre in Montmartre as a typical
tourist trap, for me, and I suspect for
others, it still has an element of magic
about it. The profusion of painters and
paintings, the well used easels set up in
the cobbled square, the pavement bistros,
with, towering over the whole scene, the
magnificent benevolence of the Church of
the Sacred Heart. It is totally Parisian
that even today one still imagines that
Toulouse Lautrec will come hobbling
through one of those doorways.*

stemmed from the far-seeing vision of a military genius. The
regularity and uniformity of design are easily linked to the strategy
of military thinking – it is of course the vastness of the concept that
impresses one. The insoluble problem of trying to impose onto an
ancient, sprawling metropolis like London, a successful traffic
highway plan, does not apply to the centre of Paris.

Was it just the 'Little General's' arrogant desire for grandeur or
did he foresee that modern society's population and transport was
going to escalate so alarmingly within two centuries? I do not
know. What does come to mind when I walk along the Champs
Elysées is the mental picture of Napoleon's very own Imperial
Guard, marching shoulder to shoulder, eight abreast, one of the
most fearsome, imposing and efficient corps of fighting men the

Church of the Sorbonne, oil on canvas
30" × 40"

world had ever seen. Was such a grand avenue conceived purely for
their victory march? Certainly such magnificent architecture would
have been justified for so great a pedestrian event.

The picture lingers and grows in my mind's eye – perhaps
thereby stems a painting!

OPPOSITE: *Rue de la Pouest*, Grasse, oil
on canvas, 30" × 20" (collection Miss
Ann Hampson)

Weathering the Storm, oil on canvas, 36″ × 24″ (collection Miss Ann Hampson)

FROM ANN HAMPSON

It was owing to my interest in Archaeology that I first 'discovered' Ben Maile. I was in Harrods when various artefacts brought up from the *Mary Rose* were being exhibited, and I was thrilled to be able to buy a signed print of the ill fated warship. I bought the print for the vessel alone but soon became fascinated by the intriguing trio of sea, sky and ship. Until then my main interest in art was limited to the works of 18th-century porcelain painters; I love colour so perhaps that explains why the porcelain delights me.

But with the print I was enjoying a new experience. I saw things which took on an added significance; the impression that the artist loves the sea, even at its most perilous, came over in strength. I found that the ominous cloud formation; the golden light reflecting a dying day, were suggestive of something more than mere gloom. I was awed by the weighty conviction of impending disaster. Perhaps my knowledge of the ship's ultimate fate strengthened these impressions, I do not know. What I did know at the time was that I wanted an original, of a sailing ship.

And there it was! I could hardly believe it when I saw it at Ben's exhibition in Harrods some time later. I was just as intrigued; the haunting quality of the saffron light, reluctant to be vanquished by the clouds; the overall tranquility which gave the impression of safety – all different from the *Mary Rose* painting and yet just as exciting.

I had decided on that, and another painting when Ben came in and we were introduced by the assistant. We had a long interesting chat after having discovered that our early struggles were similar. As we talked, I noticed a woman looking at the *Street in France* with rather more interest than I cared for; I beckoned the assistant to stick on the red dot, just to put my mind at rest.

This one attracts even more attention from my friends than the others; no one ever comes into my sitting-room without standing to stare, and to comment. It is an intriguing picture in several ways, not least of which is that it seems to possess a certain sensitivity evocative of the artist's own personal experiences and I began to wonder just what had inspired him to put brush to canvass for the creation of this one. The appealing sense of colour, and the informality set me wondering about Ben – whose character I admit I unashamedly tried to read as we talked. My excuse was that as an author, every new face is a potential character for a book. I began to wonder if there was for him some nostalgic vision of a tremendously happy and contented occasion – maybe Ben will provide me with the answer one day.

The picture holds, for me, a mystery, too. Those shadowed arches . . . what lies beyond and behind them? It is a scene alive and vital despite the tantalising arches which fill me with the desire to probe – or maybe frustration will drive me to finding that street one day! But maybe the mystery will always remain guarded, as the artist meant it to be.

It is a romantic scene, and peaceful, with those enhancing figures who are not in a hurry at all; a comforting circumstance. One would feel safe and contented in a place like that.

Altogether it is a happy picture, looking just right on my wall above a Japanese cabinet I brought all the way from Singapore. Those erudites who will throw up their hands in horror as they declare that the two do not go together, will not appreciate my reason for the combination: both were impulse buys, each having been coveted on sight; each gave me instant pleasure; so my subconcious reaction was that 'I must have it'. It was a case of first impressions, and these have never let me down.

I am very much looking forward to acquiring more of Ben Maile's paintings – I do have quite an expanse of wall space left!

MISS ANN HAMPSON
Novelist.

I know little of Yugoslavia other than some limited travel along the Dalmatian coast, but I imagine that, like London and England, New York and the U.S.A., one cannot judge the parent country by this one, fascinating city. So visit and get to know it in its own right. Let it present itself as a very substantial chunk of historical architecture, for unless you can take up residence within its walls for a few months at least, I doubt you will be able to savour to any degree its social or cultural climate. Many large cities can at the right approach open up to the stranger in their midst regardless of any language barrier, but whether it was the Yugoslavs or Dubrovniks, I found a hardening obstruction towards communication whenever I tried to pass beyond the host/tourist level of polite tolerance. A naïve, down to earth and honest approach, confessing my own inadequacies, that I had used successfully across a world of totally differing societies, carried no persuasion or conviction in Dubrovnik! So I contented myself with the visual acquaintance only, but well worth it.

Dubrovnik is a city within a city. Behind its massive ramparted walls (one of the very few remaining walled cities in Europe) the main part of the citadel is, if my memory serves me well, 15th-century – old enough to interest any historian. Here within the great fortifications are buildings, either residential or commercial now, that were minor forts themselves in their day. Climb one of the narrow laddered side-streets leading off the main thoroughfare and one goes back a further 500 years. Here, shouldering the chimneys and parapets of the later township, is still the living and lived in quarter of Dubrovnik's civilized beginnings. Here it was occupied alternatively by Saracens, Crusaders and Turks.

Caiques and dhow-type craft, now dieselized of course, plied their various trades from its shelter and once again the obvious defensive purpose of its massively constructed piers and fortifications triggered off an imagination already stimulated by the town itself. Here to this port had come the multi-oared gallies of Mussulman the Great, huge galleons from Spain and Portugal in the West. Earlier had seen the Venetians, masters of navigation, sailing long slender Craft, similar to Viking longships, into the port. Turks, Crusaders, Corsairs from the North African coast, all followed courses first made by the Roman legions of early Caesar — a vertiable cavalcade of marine history.

In the city itself, allowing for the physical division of its history, the architecture is a mixture – Byzantine, Turkish, Moorish, but all with the unmistakable Mediterranean overlay. Thank goodness those early city fathers prescribed the impregnable fortifications. They helped Dubrovnik withstand the sieges, survive the sackings and endure the ravages of time itself to preserve for to-day's traveller and particularly the curiously perceptive painter, a wealth of material and structure to view, to explore and to paint.

Dubrovnik

OVERLEAF: *A Street in Dubrovnik*, oil on canvas, 30″ × 20″

33

The Roman Colosseum, acrylic and oil, 30" × 40"

Both the Greek Parthenon and this great amphitheatre standing proudly in the centre of Rome always impress me with the sense of vast extravagance: the one paid to the Gods and the other to the cruelties and frailties of human life. Most of all, though, the sheer material extravagance in the use of stone and marble. Today the left-over or rejected stones of the Romans and Greeks would suffice to build a palatial 20th-century mansion.

But what a testimony these ruins are to their builders, a lasting proof of the immense concept and pure artistry of the designers. For all man's technology and training, in 2000 years we have seen precious few architects who can in any way approach such an imaginative creative vision of design.

These are all thoughts engendered by the sight of the exterior of the Colosseum. Enter, and the imagination seizes upon history at its bloodiest; the roar of the beasts, screams of the slaves and the clash of gladiators' combat ring in the ears.

There is of course as much violent noise just outside. Rome's never ending combat of modern traffic no doubt acts as suggestive

The Colosseum Rome

sound effects, but it is a strange and intriguing contrast. This magnificent monument to the greatest era in Roman history with its stone roots spreading out to the squalor, noise and corruption of the Rome of today.

New York To San Francisco

The American authorities do not hand out visas upon arrival the way so many European countries do. You have to make due application in advance. Having applied and received a permanent visa I arrived at Kennedy Airport *en route* for New York. I cannot profess to know that city really well. Who can? It obviously has many facets, many moods and like other cities they change with the seasons and the colours.

I first saw New York in late winter, when the colours left me with an overall impression of a variety of blues. The famous waterfront, which has to be seen from a rubber-necking water-bus or the Staten Island Ferry, was even more massive and more spectacular than the media of newsprint and television had ever done justice to.

This skyscraper panorama was a vast range of blues, greys and violets. Only the immediate shore line and dockside threw up the occasional splash of colour. The whole scene was an exercise in line and form. No indulgence in rounds and curves here. The line was severe and direct. The form was cubist, not spherical, and yet, while the whole demanded the first precepts of pure drawing, the perspective as such could not be essayed by line. There were no apparent vanishing points. It was almost as if some incredible blackcloth was supported from a thousand feet above the waterline. Yet that great vertical flatness *did* have form and depth. I sensed the bulk of the city behind it rather than saw, but it was there, and conveying it into a painting was an intriguing challenge in tonal control. All that depth suggesting a city within a city would have to be presented with an exacting treatment of differing shades upon shades of almost the same colour. That memory, the painting memory, stays with me still.

The other face of New York that appealed to me was exemplified by the painting *West Side*. It was my first meeting with the Brooklyn area of New York, and once again I saw it in a treatment of blues. I have never seen the city in summer – I wonder, would I use another, warmer range of colour? At that time, in March, the light, like the air, was cold and crisp. It filtered down through the iron fire escapes of the brownstone tenements as if it were rationed. In the late afternoon it created fantasy shapes out of the ironwork, the overhead gantries and the neon signs. On the side-walks the huge fire-hydrants hid in the steam vapour that curled up from iron gratings in the roadway. Everywhere seemed to be iron ladders, reaching upwards as if to escape the cold blue world below. It was a painting scene that one could almost fantasise with. Yet, paint as I did on one occasion, from imagination, using tonal patterns of blues and violets, then overlaying those patterns with black trellis

Approach to Manhattan, oil on canvas,
24″ × 30″ (collection Mr Ted Coupland)

TROLLEY CAR
GEARY ROAD SAN FRANCISCO

lines; block in a shape or two from outer space and finally touch in a wisp of misty vapour. What do you have? A bold abstract? Maybe. But the first observer of mine said, albeit tentatively, "Where is that – New York?"

From New York I flew direct to San Francisco. There were no impressions of abstract art here. San Francisco is a very solid material city. Yet for all its modernity one can sense a touch of its early American past. Maybe it is the elegance of some of its older opulent hotels and the occasional brick-built private house vieing proudly with the later structures of concrete and steel. Certainly its famous trolley-cars retain the atmosphere of the Nineties. Its an up and down city too. Has any other town so many hills and valleys, dips and peaks? The sight of a San Francisco trolley-car cresting the top of Union or Geary is unique throughout the States.

No doubt there are grimy back alleys in San Francisco. There must be somewhere the counterpart to New York's tenement areas, but they are not so easily found. My painting of this lively, exuberant city was in the atmosphere of its eager bustle, its movement and certainly those switchback streets with overladen trolley-cars. Then as a separate dramatic motif subject, there is the famous Golden Gate Bridge. Paint that great suspension bridge, soaring into seeming infinity and every American will instantly identify it. Just when I thought I was getting the feel of this city, the mood and atmosphere, I turned a corner and walked straight into China. Or at least San Francisco's Chinatown, which is more traditionally Chinese than parts of modern Peking – or so they say.

Where did this fit in with the unique quality that the rest of this great city had shown me? – I decided that it didn't. Yes, it was totally populated by Chinese and it had the colour, customs and noises of the Orient (whoever was it who talked of the passive enigmatic oriental?), but it had an overlay of gloss about it, a gilding of Hollywood. I decided to stay with the switchback hills and trolley-cars, the ornamental street lamps and the external elevators that glided forty floors up the outside walls of posh hotels. The really engrossing Chinese scenes I discovered much later in the backwaters of Hong Kong.

Hong Kong

Hong Kong is not perhaps the real China, but compared to the tinsel and spotlights of San Francisco's Chinatown it gives me an impression of being much nearer ancient civilization. Despite the Western influence in architecture, culture and social life, the ladder streets of Kowloon are unmistakably Oriental.

A drive southwards across the island to beautiful Repulse Bay is a direct step back into a Somerset Maugham setting. There, just across to Aberdeen Harbour, is Hong Kong at its native best.

The pretty young girl in traditional river, folk garb and wide-brimmed coolie hat persuaded me to take a sampan trip around the harbour, and then deposited me in an ancient, unstable, smelly little craft, piloted by a toothless old man who looked like a wizened baboon dressed up for a tea advertisement. 'Oh well, another sucker taken for a ride,' thought I – but I wanted to find some atmosphere, didn't I? An hour later, I had really found it.

Deposited back on the massive great parent junk – a floating home for five families – I has persuaded the 'Brooke Bond Baboon' to let me take up station on the family deck and continue sketching. Well, his English was virtually non-existent, so I stayed anyway, pulling out a few extra dollar notes when I thought appropriate. I considered the small bribe well worthwhile, for mine was an excellent vantage point.

The whole fascinating harbour lay before me. Various callers arrived while I sat and sketched. The greengrocer, the butcher, the pots and pans man, and someone whom I guessed was the local rent collector. All arrived by boat and the attendant noise and bustle, colour and movement, was a painter's dream. In any other setting the noise would have been no help at all to intense sketching, but here it was all part of the atmosphere.

From arrival at Kai Tak right through our entire stay in Hong Kong, the noise was a never-ending background to all human activity. The people of Hong Kong seem to be the most impulsive, vociferous and argumentative I have ever met.

The visiting greengrocer and Senior *Madame* on the junk who did the buying exchanged such a frenzy of verbal repartee that it seemed impolite for me, a Westerner, to observe it. But, their bartering completed, they shook hands several times, beamed toothless smiles and greengrocer-san was introduced to me with much bowing and scraping and friendly goodwill. His obvious interest in my activity prompted me to give him the sketch I had done on his arrival. His gratitude was out of all proportion, and I accepted only one large and succulent melon from the fruit he offered me. The melon joined the family feast I was later to join. I was still reflecting on the greengrocer's meeting when the wizened baboon reappeared laden with plastic bags.

When he had asked, as I thought, for cigarettes, and I had given him the assumed tip, plus an extra dollar or two and loudly shouted (he *had* to be deaf at such an advanced age) "Beer – Beer," he had fled, presumably to spend his ill-gotten gains. Now here I was presented with two packets of cigarettes, a carton of canned beer and some small change! Oh ye of little faith! I presented him with the cigarettes to smoke (I am a non-smoker) and invited him to join me with a beer – he must have thought I was some indulgent genie. His incredulous thanks and enjoyment were something to behold.

ABERDEEN HONG KONG

Aberdeen Harbour,
Hong Kong, water
colour 22″ × 31″

40

Kowloon Hong Kong

By the time the afternoon tradesmen had arrived and departed and wizened baboon had taken me off on the sampan around the harbour again (no charge this time) introducing me to all and sundry and the beer packs were depleted to one can, I was feeling as mellow and benevolent as wizened baboon was feeling important. When we got back to the home junk the children (nearly all girls), fifteen of them (if the beer did not upset the counting), were arriving home from school. Gleaming and spotless, with white blouses and grey skirts and identical little satchels, they would have been a credit to any English institute of education.

Their ages, guessed, ranged from seven to fifteen, and they were all made to file past me with a shy smile, a giggle and a nervous bob of the head in acknowledgement.

Later, joining them around the huge communal dining-table, they were made to practise their school taught English on the 'gwailo' stranger.

As I shared the excellent meal of rice and various seafoods contained in two gigantic woks I thought of the turgid water surrounding us that served as a receptacle and provider for everything. I thought of Jane's (my daughter) strict admonishment, "Whatever you do, Dad, don't drink anything unless its from a can, and *don't eat anything* in Aberdeen." Jane had lived in Hong Kong for five years and she knew all the hazards. As I reflected on this I realised my friendly little schoolgirls were translating some advice from my harbour hosts.

"This is good food," they were telling me — I agreed — it was splendid food. "It is freshly caught and all cleaned and cooked here by us. *But* whatever painter-san does, he mustn't eat at the Mandarin's Palace." The shaking of heads and appropriate solemn looks on the Chinese features emphasized the warning. I hastily assured them I had no intention of eating at the Manderin's Palace.

This establishment was a colossal floating restaurant at the tourist end of the harbour, resplendent with scarlet and golden dragons decorating its entrance. Magnificent pagoda-style roof and gilded balconies enticed one to peer through the windows. Its opulent interior would have done justice to any of San Francisco's Chinese establishments, as was evidenced by the clutches of American tourists succumbing to its blatant charms. But I was no fool. If the natives didn't know a good restaurant from a bad one, who did? No, my smelly, overpopulatd, leaky old junk was a far better eating-house.

When I returned from my adventures complete with a full sketch-book and a full stomach later that evening, to the modern hygienic comfort of my daughter's air-conditioned apartment, she turned pale with anxiety when I related the events of the day. It must have been a full three days before she relaxed her nervous vigilance. Funny, I was quite all right, not even a mild indigestion.

My Aberdeen hosts had expected a return visit from me, but my own family were convinced that only a miracle had saved me from cholera or worse, and their anxiety would not allow the hazard of another visit to Aberdeen.

It was not until the last morning before flying out that I stole down there again. I stood out of sight and watched the crocodile of well-remembered little girls filing off the junk to head for school.

From the concealing shadows of an old building I watched the waterborne tradesmen arrive and start their noisy delivery of supplies – the wizened baboon appeared and climbed into his little sampan after exchanging noisy insults (greetings? who ever knew?) with the tradesmen, motored off down river, creating rippled reflections on the muddy water. I watched him disappear into a sunny haze of early morning light and took one last, long look at the watery shadows and reflections, at all the boats, junks and barges, at the rattan canopies and faded canvas awnings, holding stubbornly out against another day's scorching sun.

I looked, watched and remembered against the time when I would need to repeat them in my own way, with my canvas and paint.

St. Katherine's Dock/Don Quixote

This painting ·may not seem the most obvious to fill a spot between the colourful scenes of Hong Kong and the highly imaginative painting of Don Quixote. Strangely it does play a justifiable role as a 'link' in time. Most of my earlier scenes of the Thames and London's dockland had originated some years before, and when work was started, replanning and rebuilding my favourite area between Tower Bridge and Puddle Dock, I had deplored the first sight of some ghastly 20th-century architecture. I kept away for a long time, preferring my memories of the old dockside to the hideous replacements.

Just before leaving for Hong Kong, I was visiting some friends in the shipping business at the newly refurbished Ivory House. One of them took me around the dock. Some of the now finished 20th-century architecture was still ghastly, but the dock itself was fascinating. A large part of it devoted to marine museum use in the best possible taste which was captivating for anyone at all interested in ships, boats and things to do with the sea. I was a total devotee to it all.

The old warehouses carefully reconstructed were living once again and formed a graceful background for the inner dock whilst the old Dickens Eating House, taken to pieces at the initial reconstruction and then painstakingly rebuilt, was a joy to behold as well as a joy to enter. The bar with its floor of sawdust still supporting 300 year old pillars and beams of English oak, redeemed any accusations of sacrilege. I thought I knew my London well. However it was a humbling experience to be introduced to such a gem on the Thames, by someone who, when I was last sketching in the area, had been a young boy! Whatever the reasons I spent a few days there filling a sketch book once again.

Now the scene and the time changes, by a few months, to Geelong, near Melbourne, Australia. Preparing for an exhibition there in the Balmoral Gallery in that township I was finalising the last of the canvases to be catalogued. Although it had been the wide range of my successful prints that had prompted the initial invitation to exhibit, the agent responsible was worried that typical Ben Maile London scenes might not appeal. We were after all discussing commercial success not just aesthetic satisfaction. "You should paint some gum trees," said my 'Aussie' agent, quite seriously. "The Aussies love their gum trees." So I painted some gum trees. It was a good exercise, there's always something to learn in a new subject. Afterwards though I went back to my London sketchbook.

A lot of work had been sent over in advance but I was spending a couple of months in a makeshift studio adding some extra stock. The brilliant light and the beautiful blue-grey tones of the tree covered hills all around me, gave a new dimension to whatever I painted. To the north some 6 or 7 miles away on the skyline the lovely Dandenong range of mountains stretched. From here too gum trees of every variety and size abounded in profusion. (Only 3

St Katherine's Dock, oil on canvas, 20″ × 24″ (collection B. D. Taylor)

Ben working in the studio at Wonga Park, near Melbourne

years later the terrible epidemic of bush fires ravaged this beautiful landscape.) The beauty of this scenery had been superbly portrayed by that doyen of Australian artists, Hans Heysen. When I remembered the enduring quality of his canvases I abandoned my gum trees.

The historic old gold mining area at Sovereign Hill near Ballarat gave me more substance to build on in the familiar Ben Maile technique, and such a scene presented the largest painting in the exhibition. One of the smallest came from my London sketch-book – *St. Katherine's Dock* – and despite my agent's fears, it was one of the first to receive a red seal.

A week before the exhibition was due to open, after all the framing and mounting and cataloguing was agreed, I felt the urge to produce just one more work. Something different, and arresting. By this time, I had adjusted to the unique quality of the highly purifying light of Victoria and was even experimenting with colours I would not have used back home in England. Sarah, my young grandaughter who was attending the Royal Melbourne Ballet School, was inquistively thumbing through an old sketch-book of mine. She suddenly lighted upon some very rough, scribbled sketches I has worked on years before. Cervantes' tragi-romantic hero, had long fascinated me, a definitive yet impressionist painting of the character would hopefully depict all the pathos, tragedy and loneliness implicit in the legend and was a great temptation.

Before I had taken the sketches any further one of the popular artists of the day had produced a very competent depiction of the character which had appeared in art print form. Its appearance nipped my ideas in the bud and I didn't want to be thought guilty of

FROM BILL OWEN

It was the annual Ben Maile Exhibition at the Dorchester Hotel, which that year was mainly concerned with paintings after his visit to Venice.

Perhaps I should explain at this point that I am neither an expert nor a connoisseur of art, and I am not sure that I could put into words my reasons for acquiring the 'Ben Mailes' that adorn my walls.

Being a regular visitor to Ben's exhibitions I amble around casually, but always hoping there will be one that will 'stop me in my tracks'.

So it was that evening. It was unexpected. It bore no connection to any other painting on show and the subject and execution gave no indication of Ben. The fact that I am an actor and the subject being theatrical may have been responsible for my immediate reaction. But it was the sheer majesty of the work that had me almost mesmerised. The 'Dreaming of the impossible dream' of Don Quixote, was all there on that canvas, so I stayed and I stared, for how long I don't know. If there was one 'Ben Maile' I would like to own it would be *Don Quixote*! But I know that it isn't possible, so all I can hope is that Ben will 'stop me in my tracks' with another such subject, in the not too distant future.

MR. BILL OWEN, M.B.E.
Actor, Film, Stage and Television.

plagiarism. But now, some years afterwards, young Sarah had re-kindled my enthusiasm. It appeared that Sir Robert Helpman had visited Melbourne shortly before with his choreographed ballet version of the *Man from Le Mancha*. In no time with the excitement of the truly young, Sarah produced stage photos of the perform-ance, reviews and copies of the costume design. All was jubilation. My grandaughter, bless her, had sparked off the fires of inspiration. A few amendments to my old sketches, the introduction of the windmills, which had always worried me, was solved in a flash. Just suggest the windmill sails, broken to the ground as if Quixote had tilted at them – and for once thought he had conquered.

This painting, which had been lying dormant, nagging at me, for some five years or more, was now given life. A large canvas was set up and in three days of fierce frenetic painting it was completed. Sarah's first action on arrival home from school in the evenings was to visit the studio and inspect progress. Our pride in its completion was mutually shared.

It too was received well at the exhibition previews and would have been carried off along with *St. Katherine's Dock, Sovereign Hill* and others, had I not affixed the 'not for sale' tag to it. *Don Quixote* had been too long in its gestation, too deeply shared by the family, to be relinquished. As I write he commands the wall behind me, still surveying those down-fallen sails as if still dubious of conquest.

So Hong Kong had delayed the oil painting of St. Katherine's Dock; perhaps Aberdeen Harbour, forming a similar yet contrast-ing scene, helped establish a keener view-point when the old London scenes recurred, and, this in turn was a stepping stone to Don Quixote.

Conceived in England, given birth in Australia, and now hang-ing, pride of place, in our Cornwall home.

Australia
Port Fairy: Western Victoria

Port Fairy is a product of the early gold rush days of Australia and as such has its own quota of tales of drama and tragedy. My eye and my sketch-book were captured by this rugged piece of architecture that graphically expresses the pioneering spirit that prevailed in those days. To the modern view-point it may seem very basic, but listen to what the local press had to say of its opening " . . . the largest hotel in the Western District, boasting an elegant and lofty saloon 60 feet in length and admirably suited for balls, concerts and public entertainments. A covered balcony running along two sides of the hotel for about 180 feet affords an agreeable promenade . . ."

That 'agreeable promenade', at a time when the town was a political constituency of some significance, also afforded the politi-cians of the day a splendid platform for electioneering speeches. Looking at it today, silent and seemingly deserted, it is hard to imagine the vibrant life that must have filled and surrounded it.

Perhaps the most significant feature of this cameo of Australian history is the fact that its builder and owner, one John Walwyn

Star of the West, Port Fairy, oil on canvas, 20″ × 24″

Taylor, was a native emigrant from the West Indies. For a black Jamaican to come into a very macho society as this in the year 1856 when racial discrimination was an accepted rule, underlines that he must have been a character of considerable strength and style.

The information one accumulates when setting out to paint a picture of an old pub!

Interested emus being sketched near Ballarat, Australia

An overnight stop – maybe a couple of days stay. I had never been here before, but that was the original intention with our arrival at this much talked of city. How blasé can one get! A week later we were still there running out of time and planning a return.

Eroding into the lagoon it may be, though it is not easy to find obvious signs of decay in Venice; for a city steeped in a thousand years of history its architecture may be crumbling in places, but it's still commanding, elegant in shape, timeless in character.

My first sight of St. Mark's Square was on a moonlit evening, and the total romance of the scene was such that it could have been a three dimensional stage setting. I was almost reluctant to walk across it, by moonlight the next evening, for fear of anticlimax, but there was no betrayal; that lavish balconied, palatial stage of history sustained its magical impact every time.

The architects of the day had been given a splendid brief, costings were the least consideration and they had portrayed their imaginative skills with courage and vision. The results, when completed, must have fulfilled their every expectation, but surely not even they could have foreseen the breathtaking tricks that moonlight would

Venice

St Mark's Square at Night, oil on canvas, 28″ × 36″

49

Saluté Palace, Venice, oil on canvas, 28″ × 36″

SALUTÈ   VENICE

Saluté Palace from the Gritti, oil on canvas, 36″ × 48″

play with shape and shadows and even colour.

I still want to paint my ultimate Venice scene: St. Mark's, under that same moonlight with the whole Square a challenge of blues, greys and silvers and every column, archway and shuttered window masquarading in tinted shadows.

I visited the square again early next morning when sluggish diesel barges were furrowing the lagoon's surface to deliver the day's supplies to hotel, store and café. How different in the high, morning light.

The pigeons, unseen before, were a moving carpet across the vast square, breaking into long flying skeins to join up to the top of the Campanile, and then sweeping across to reach the marble horses above the doorway of the Cathedral itself. Yet even they in their thousands were lesser creatures, still dwarfed by the whole spatial design.

From the Square I walked through to the harbour front. The waters of the lagoon (and what an inadequate title) were picture postcard blue, and the silky black gondolas were jibbing like restless horses at the mooring posts. Their gondoliers, straw boatered and striped shirted, were only just arriving, and if last night's scene had been Shakespearean this was pure Gilbert & Sullivan.

St Mark's Square and the Campanile, oil on canvas 28″ × 36″

So bedazzled was I with the magic of Venice that this notice of an exhibition of paintings of Europe must have puzzled many visitors when they arrived and discovered it was virtually an exhibition of Venice.

I decided there and then that this was a city that needed a three month stay at least, and, with the magnificent light that was a painter's dream, a stay that would include a wide-windowed studio as well.

Though I have revisited Venice, each time has been too short; that three month stay and the studio is not yet. Perhaps one day. . . .

THE GOLDEN SQUARE – INNSBRUCK

An absolute tourist spot. The square, seemingly, where everyone who visits Innsbruck all gather together with the local population to enjoy the near-ritual of gâteaux, pastries and coffee in the pre-lunch hours. The palace with the golden roof, or more specifically with the golden roofed balcony (large balcony, large roof), built by some indulgent royal for his bride-to-be, dominates the square and deserves to. It is a remarkable building, the famous roof regularly re-gilded with genuine gold leaf and the whole front is decorated with delightful plaster frescos. A fairy-tale background, commercial exposure and exploitation, questionable function, but nevertheless the whole finished effect is one of benevolent charm. Sit at an open-air café in the square, sipping hot rich coffee, nibbling at one of their delicious apfelstrudel pastries and try not to feel indulgent and warm-hearted. The Austrian gregariousness is infectious and with all the different nationalities around, the world becomes your cousin. There is no doubt that those glinting golden reflections from that magic roof are having a benevolent effect on everyone.

The Golden Square, Innsbruck, oil on canvas (collection Mr David Nixon)

Innsbruck

Basically the architecture here is Gothic but with an overlay of gilding and decoration that I feel must be due to the lighter, more extrovert nature of the Austrians, so distinctly noticeable after leaving the more austere outlook of their German neighbours.

It was the older, narrow side-streets that attracted my eye. The high walls of severe masonry with their deep shuttered windows rising steeply from the narrow cobbled streets, were, with the lack of any pavements, almost claustrophobic. Inhibiting to walk through, hazardous to drive through, but with the sunlight breaking through the far end, throwing into sharp relief the first-floor balconies with their wrought iron rails and emphasising the steep pitch of the roofs, the whole narrow, forbidding alley became a painter's delight.

Deep shadows, sharp contrast of light, blurred, mystic outlines in the distance and the exciting challenge of subtle tones allied with distinct form in the foreground presented an immediate exercise of one's visual perception.

I can go back and find equally absorbing but subtly different studies each time I visit this proud old town looking across the Inn valley towards the Italian frontier with its background of snow-capped Austrian Alps – for all the world like some mammoth painted theatrical backcloth.

From Innsbruck to Sidi Bou Said

It is interesting to speculate upon the mood – the painting mood that is – aroused by the scene. While enthusiasm is always awakened by a new scene, the mood, reaction and treatment varies so much with the subject.

Some years ago, when I 'discovered' Innsbruck for the first time, it left me with sufficient material to keep me painting for months. Starting off with the famous Golden Square, I had explored, with sketch-book and camera, every little side street and alleyway that the district had to offer. It was all very much to my particular taste. Structurally heavy and dramatic, even sombre in places, but intriguingly counter-balanced, with painted plaster frescos and gilded hanging signs. The whole scene fitted admirably into my favourite palette. The umbers and ochres and that beautiful, strong Italian pink – which isn't actually pink at all. Cavernous Gothic doorways, black oak beams and many toned shadows absorbed my painting for months.

My next trip abroad after this took me to Tunisia. What a contrast! I can spend a sunny day in Innsbruck and the shadows and tonal subtleties created around those old buildings are even more enhanced. But in North Africa, with a sunlight seemingly from a different spectrum, there is far less subtlety. The contrasts are more marked and the shadows are hard and sharp. To begin with, I felt that this scene was not for me at all. Not so much because of the lack of subtlety, but by reason of the overall immensely high key to everything. I had always worked in a much lower key, preferring

Street in Innsbruck, oil on canvas, 30″ × 20″ (collection Mr Ted Coupland)

Early Morning, Sidi Bou Said, Tunisia, watercolour, 22″ × 15″

my lights to be emphasised by the darks. Showing a smaller but striking flash of sunlight framed by a perspective of long street lamp for instance, awakened the gloom and shadows of surrounding buildings. In Tunisia though it was all light all the time. Sensibly I obeyed my own dictum and decided not to try to paint or sketch at all – yet. I just looked and went on looking.

With my wife and friends we took a hired car, a bouncing little Spanish thing, and set about exploring. We found Naboul, the centuries old oasis town marking the nomadic caravan route. It was truly Biblical in appearance with spice market, camel market, herbs, leathers, fat dates and fly-blown meat. Here, unlike the city dwellers, even the men kept a male equivalent of the yashmak about their features as we approached.

The onset of the camera in my wife's hands clearly upset them, but my sketch-book, provoked at last by this primitive scene, seemed only to intrigue them. When I look at some of those old sketches now I can almost smell the heady spices and hear the peculiar chanting of the camel boys.

Sidi Bou Said

Even more spectacular were the old souks of Sousse. Seemingly subterranean market places, that shut out that fierce sunlight and invited one inside to a vista of colour, hazy shadows and an atmosphere of intriguing, ancient mystery. Here indeed were subjects that I could – and did – paint without that all-encompassing wash of strong light. Even so it meant an excursion into a less familiar palette. The cadmium reds and yellows were called for here as were the ultramarines and violets, where before I had used coeruleum blue and raw umber.

This all served well in coming to terms with the question of light. So it was fortuitous timing that we did not find Sidi Bou Said until the end of our trip. We had driven off to visit the ancient city of Carthage. It was the one tribute to orthodox tourism that I was prepared to make, but a wasted tribute. The much vaunted historical remains are a sad reflection of man's careless neglect. Sidi Bou Said, however, more than made up for that disappointment.

Perched a few miles away on top of the cliffs above the sea, with its one cobbled main street wandering down to a picturesque

Sunlight and Shadows in Sidi Bou Said, watercolour, 22″ × 15″

60

fishing harbour, it could, in features perhaps, be termed an Arabian St. Ives. In substance it was so different. The buildings were exquisite. Small, but beautifully proportioned with pristine white walls and vivid blue woodwork. Elegant panelled doors, painstakingly made by the finest of artisan craftsmen, were suspended on massive, wrought-iron black hinges. Others bore symmetrical patterns of hexagonal iron studs, again black. The wrought-iron was repeated in delicately fashioned grills, sometimes over the doors and windows, sometimes part of them. Then there were the balconies also with their iron railings and hung with heavy hand-woven rugs.

So there was this breath-taking scene, all bright blue and white with its black tracings. Elegant and very private houses stepping one above the other to the top of the hill. On one side of the climbing street was a brief interlude. A domestic supply of fruiterers, greengrocers and butchers, but compared to Sousse and Naboul, more of Kensington quality than Aldgate. This gave the brief but telling contrast of bright warm colours against the hard blues and sheer whites that tended to dominate.

With the previous Tunisian scenes, the people as much as the place had fed my imagination, the hustle and bustle of Arab gowns, turbans and tarbooshes. The veils and yashmaks and hard stares of totally alien faces had all served to create that certain something that we call atmosphere. Here, though, in Sidi Bou Said it was the fine graceful architecture that dominated and indicated the character of its inhabitants as well. The few people we did meet were courteous but not ingratiating, proud but not haughty. And so the atmosphere slowly formed. Buildings and people had less colour and movement than the souks and camel markets but still with their very own, almost elusive quality. Here high on the cliff tops with the added factor of sea reflected sunlight, it was a provoking challenge. Paint this – paint me.

Detail of door Sidi Bou Said

London

Edwardian London

The first discovery of some foreign city is always exciting. My first visit to Paris was so stimulating that I have been revisiting it for years and it never fails to be a delightful capital. San Francisco has an excitement and atmosphere all its own. Not so easily reached as Paris, and probably looked forward to with more anticipation because of that. And Venice – what a city of dreams! There is no other quite like it.

Those are probably my favourite foreign cities. Yet, when I come to London, which is often enough to wear thin any novelty, I realise that this vast, sprawling, untidy metropolis has a quality of difference that none of the others can match. To be truthful, my feelings for London are a sort of love/hate emotion. I hate its grime and untidiness, the traffic and the diesel fumes, and being an ex-Londoner, I resent the apparent take-over of the place by every nationality, bar the English. Its uncaringness for its own kind appals me, yet, knowing it well, I can find its quiet peaceful

Snowstorm over St Paul's, oil on canvas, 28" × 36"

corners. There are streets I can walk with my sketch-book that I know I could not walk were it some other city. Yet its overall attraction is in its history. Since the days of the Romans and right through to the influence of Wren it has acquired a character that somehow makes it seem inviolate.

I well remember arriving home on leave late at night in wartime, in the middle of an air raid. I looked at London in daylight, ravaged, smoking and covered in acres of meaningless debris, and watched bewildered cockney families, for whom their world had seemed to end. But London survived. It even survived the equally cruel onslaught by so called designers and architects when they started rebuilding the city. But St Paul's is still there. Try as they might with their glass and concrete columns they cannot subdue that superb piece of architecture.

The Law Courts and Fleet Street are there too. The various Inns of Court spread like a maze with their 17th-century courtyard gardens only a few steps from the hustle and bustle of Temple Bar. In there, one is transported instantly into a world that seems centuries away. The Thames, incredibly, has actually been de-

FROM VINCE HILL
There is a saying in the art world that you should never meet the artist, particularly if it is someone whose work you have really admired for years. In your mind he or she has been on a pedestal – someone touched by God with a very special talent – and when you meet it can often be a shattering disappointment. Well, I met Ben and his wife Barbara when I was on board the Blenheim cruising round the Canaries. I was doing the cabaret for a couple of weeks and Ben was very complimentary about my work – you would have thought he knew I owned one of his paintings! But seriously, it gave me an opportunity to meet and talk to this man whose picture still has pride of place in our house after all these years and if the saying is true about meeting artists, then Ben is the exception to the rule.

MR VINCE HILL
Singer

The Cheshire Cheese, Fleet Street

polluted, but can still give you a boatride through 500 years of history. Yes, the capital may be a tourist dilemma, and a commuter's nightmare, but it still offers the painter a canvas rich in character, history and atmosphere.

St Paul's I must have painted a score of times, and I will go on painting it indefinitely. That marvellous cathedral provides a hundred different viewpoints and its mood and majesty change with the light and the weather in the way that the whole city changes with the seasons.

If I thumb through the sketch-books I have used over the years, I see cobbled mews and elegant squares, Nash terraces and tumble-down riverside wharves. Impressive Georgian pubs with collan-aded porticos and black beamed pubs that have been swinging their signs since the days of Raleigh and Pepys. When I turn a page I find detailed drawings of wrought ironwork and lamps. Those beautiful Victorian lamps along the Embankment and around Parliament

Tower Bridge, oil on canvas,
24″ × 36″

Square, have been a strong support or focal point in many of my paintings. There are sketches of new and old buildings – mostly old and riverside sketches of buildings and houses now gone forever. Sketches of quiet, 'cottagey' corners that look like little villages, which they were in the days when the city was

Trafalgar Square, watercolour, 15" × 20"

surrounded by a cluster of hamlets and villages. Many have since been swallowed up in the great urban spread, yet they still live on – the quiet corners still exist. Five minutes from the violence of Paddington Station the sketch-book finds 'Little Venice' – hardly that exotic city in miniature, but certainly seeming to be a flashback to a mid-19th-century country canal scene.

In London, one can travel with Queen Elizabeth I. You can tread the steps where Nelson was finally brought ashore after Trafalgar, drink an ale at the very bar where Dr. Johnson drank his, and lean against a wall that a Roman Centurian guarded before Christ was born. If you want to feel the lifeblood of the City, take a boat trip down the river from Westminster to Greenwich. As you draw away from Big Ben and the Parliament buildings – yet another sketch – and prepare for the history to follow, just bear in mind that those waters carrying you along are the very same that saw this city built when it was called Lud and then Londinium.

Tide in, tide out you are riding the same old river that has watched her city grow and change, from century to century. That is the pulse of London that always tugs at my sketch-book like a magnet.

St Paul's from Blackfriars
OPPOSITE. *Westminster*

FROM SIR ARTHUR BRYAN

We at Wedgwood have observed with great interest over recent years the growing success and following of the accomplished artist, Ben Maile, who has forged his own special place in the impressionist style.

A selection of the Ben Maile water-colour paintings illustrated here will form the basis of a special series of Wedgwood plates to be marketed in limited edition in 1985. The reproduction of this work in ceramics offers a difficult technical challenge but I am confident that we shall succeed in making an exciting product for Wedgwood collectors.

Chairman and Managing Director
Wedgwood plc.

Trumpeters of the Household Cavalry
All watercolours for Wedgwood Limited Edition, China Plate Design

Mevagissey Harbour, oil on canvas 36″ × 24″

Return to Cornwall

The mixed emotions that accompany me in London always sort themselves out by the time I get back to Cornwall.

Once west of the Tamar Bridge the slower pace of life gives me more time to appreciate the gorgeous scenery around me and to wonder why those cities must become so frenetic. If anyone ever wants to calm their shattered nerves or to be reassured that there is still a peaceful way of life, then just take a sketch-book and visit some of the little Cornish harbours where stout little fishing boats and the tolerant Cornish fishermen wait calmly for the next tide. If you want excitement you can experience that as well and watch those same little fishing boats battle homewards through an immense Atlantic swell.

OPPOSITE: *Crabber at Rest*, watercolour for Wedgwood Limited Edition, China Plate Design

Fishers at Newlyn,
Cornwall, oil on
canvas, 28″ × 36″
(Artist's collection)

The Tops'l Schooner, oil on canvas, 30″ × 20″

The very first 'Tops'l Schooner' sailed into Newquay harbour and into my painting world many years ago – I have been finding and painting them ever since.

MOUSEHOLE

Sea Fret and Schooners, oil on canvas, 24″ × 20″

Scottish Wild Life

L̲ike many people with vulnerable emotions and lively imaginations, I have, over the years, had cause to think deeply upon man's attitudes and treatment of his fellow animals.

Since living in Cornwall the family has had its full quota of injured or deserted birds or mammals being brought into the house and upsetting the family routine, but it was not until the awful days of the *Torey Canyon* disaster that the feelings became very strong and questioning.

Helping to organize the North Cornwall Sea Bird Rescue Centre I experienced my share of unbelievable remorse, dejection and feelings of guilt. We had over 30,000 sea birds of all descriptions passed through our hands and quite a few mammals including seals and a fox. One was bound to become a willing contributor to

The Hon. Angus Ogilvy and Ben signing Scottish Wild Life proofs

The Blackcock, watercolour

OPPOSITE: *The Badger* and *The Otter* All from the Scottish Wild Life series of watercolours

74

Angus Ogilvy presenting Ben with a token of appreciation at Sothebys

authentic animal charities after such an experience. I became even more cynical of the part man plays when I was pressured into accepting an invitation in America to participate in an art expo that was primarily to assist the causes of animal conservation. I discovered that much of their money was raised through mammoth raffles in which the prizes were game hunting safari holidays in Africa. I vowed to give that one a miss in the future, and closely examine any other animal charities.

To my embarrassment a little while later I was expounding strongly my views on the hypocrisy of some so-called animal conservation groups to the Hon. Angus Ogilvy at a luncheon party. My host hastened to explain – too late – that the Queen's cousin was patron of the Scottish Wild Life Society and had hoped that I might be persuaded to help his funds!

The man himself was charming over my boorish gaffe and eventually I was able to assist a really genuine cause.

MINES, RIGS AND PIPELINES

English China Clays

Every visitor to Cornwall sees at some time evidence of this, the one and only major production industry in the Duchy. Whereas at one time Cornwall's tin and copper was sought the world over, now only the rich, white clay – base for cosmetics, paper coatings and insulations – is the one mineral product that reaps rich export rewards. Mined and shipped out from south-eastern Cornwall, it betrays its origins by leaving high, rounded pyramids of cement-like waste. At the foot of these piles invariably lie small lakes and pools, flooded and coloured an odd shade of milky blue. The whole effect resembles a miniature, artificial Alpine scene. Small wonder perhaps that my first reaction to the sugestion of painting the clay mines was rather negative. Barry Grime, Engineering Director of the Company, was patiently tolerant of my ignorant, non-enthusiasm and eventually persuaded me at least to view the scene in more detail.

The engineering side itself was most impressive, both separation plant and refining, but of course it was the actual production that drew my interest. The open cast pit with its railed incline leading some 150 feet to the bottom – a vast expanse of hard-packed mineral clay. J.C.B.'s, bulldozers and various tracked vehicles looked from the top like an army of miniature ants carrying away their spoils, but the central feature was the battery of monitors, those powerful, high-pressure water cannon that hosed the clay from the rockface.

Yet this was stimulating. Surely some of the scenes could be painted? The palette worried me a little though. The overall colours were greys and whites with the only contrast being the hard yellows of the tractors and bulldozers. My doubts showed until one of E.C.L.P.'s senior mine captains, George Stark, divined my problem. "Let's take him down the pit at night," said George. "Everything will look different then." And it did. Under powerful sodium floodlights and even in moonlight the whole content changed colourwise. Those stark whites and greys vanished, the quartz and feldspars gave off magical colours and reflections and the probing water-jets played spectrum games of their very own.

Older, wise and experienced, Captain George, like a thousand Cornish mine-workers before him, had seen and appreciated this unique beauty long before the idea of Ben Maile painting it was mooted. As he told me later, he had wished for years that he could have put brush to paper to capture 'un'. Barry Grime had been very perceptive in putting me in the care of his senior captain on my visit. Then and on other subsequent visits I became very indebted to this quite remarkable character.

I began to see this industry which he, George, had worked in since a boy and was devoted to, through his eyes – with his vision. I thought then that I possessed a trained observer's eye, but George opened mine to another dimension. He was a big powerful man who looked capable of extracting the clay with his own hands if all else failed. Quite fearless yet totally safe and reliant he scared the pants off me one day by taking a short cut in the four wheel drive Land Rover we were using straight over the edge of a newly opened

The Hoseman, acrylic and oil, 24″ × 48″ (collection Mr Barry Grime, English China Clays)

pit and careering to the bottom in perfect if hair-raising control. He twinkled those brilliant blue eyes at me, "There – thass a mite quicker than going all the way round."

George, the gentle and generous giant of a man, was typical of that certain breed of men who seem to find their enjoyable niche in the hazardous world of mining, construction and exploration.

FROM BARRY GRIME

I regret to say that it was not until 1965 that I became aware of Ben's work. I happened casually to stroll into his small gallery overlooking the harbour at Newquay. I browsed around, liked what I saw, and was particularly impressed by a tin mining scene and then became intrigued when I realised that none of his pictures featured Cornwall's china clay industry. Without revealing my own connection, I asked why. I well recall his casual reply – "There's nothing worth painting." Of course, I swallowed the bait and personally supervised Ben's visit, in the depths of winter, to a working pit on the night shift. It didn't take him long to see the potential, although all he said to me – rather grudgingly – was "H'm, there might be something there after all!"

The result was some seven paintings depicting the winning and working of china clay. For me, one of the most striking of the day scenes is that featuring the overburden removal in readiness for mining around the wild moors surrounding Longstones & Littlejohns. The machines in use, twenty years ago, were quite large even by today's standards, and Ben captured the scale of the operation, and, of course, reminded us all of the rehabilitation job that lay ahead of us. Equally notable to me are those paintings which show the hoseman working under floodlights, controlling high pressure water jets used to break up the virgin granite matrix from which clay is derived. Two of these are amongst my very treasured possessions.

So commenced a friendship which has enabled me to admire Ben, not only as a painter, but also as a hard working and lively contributor, in a variety of ways, to the community in which he has come to live.

MR B. M. GRIME
Director, English Clays Lovering
Pochin & Co. Ltd.

Longstones Pit, acrylic and oil, 30″ × 54″ (collection Mr Barry Grime, English China Clays)

B.P. Forties

"It's not what you know – it's who you know" (I don't know the origins of that cliché, but the truth of it has been proved to me more than once).

Well, I knew Bill Owen, the Bill Owen of the 'Compo' guise, from 'The Last of the Summer Wine'. We were spending a very satisfying hour testing the merits of a malt whisky together. As we discussed art, the theatre and life in general Bill returned to the subject of art. "Ben," he said, "you paint so many different subjects and themes – which was very true – is there anything you haven't painted – something you would really like to paint?"

I puzzled over this. It was a complimentary question the way Bill put it. I told him somewhat hesitantly that I thought I would like to paint an oil rig. He appeared flabbergasted. An oil rig! Why would I want to paint an oil rig? I warmed to my subject. After all I had glimpsed them on television (or were they studio mockups?). Man-made structures towering into a dramatic sky and being lashed by massive seas.

Think of it. Puny man building steel towers out in mid ocean, pitting his technological skills and his physical prowess against the aquatic might of nature.

I made a good case of my argument, I could see that. Bill was impressed and the malt was a good one. "You really want to paint an oil rig?" I did. "O.K.," he said, "I'll fix it."

What connections Compo could have with a far-distant oil rig I had no idea – and I am still unsure. But, at the time, I had great faith in him and it was not misplaced.

I had a brief phone call from Bill a week or so later telling me to ring a certain London number. Bill's connections had arranged for me a meeting with a leading executive of the mighty B.P. Company. The timing was very fortunate. They had, it appeared, been considering the commissioning of an artist to record scenes of their North Sea Forties Field, then being set up. One attempt at this exercise had already been made, with not totally favourable results, it seemed, and a Board Room decision was pending. My entry on the scene was viewed quite fairly, but obviously critically. When I assured them that I was not desirous of a formal commission in the normal sense, but I was prepared to paint if the scene inspired me, leaving the results for them to judge, without any commitment or obligation, it appeared to be the ideal solution.

About three weeks later, after visiting Britannic House, B.P.'s headquarters, and being briefed technically upon the purpose of oil rigs in general and B.P.'s own in particular, I presented myself at the helicopter port at Aberdeen. I was equipped with everything necessary (by courtesy of B.P.) for a three weeks' stay in the Forties Field, and had added a bottle of Scotch as an arrival gift to my platform host. (My education was already starting – platform, not rig.) Further instant education – the platforms are 'dry'; no alcohol is allowed. Also, what I had not brought was my passport. I had not realized that one 'went foreign' when visiting those far distant industrial scenes! Officialdom unbent. Immigration decided that I could be permitted to leave Scottish shores provided my passport

OPPOSITE: *Heavy weather at Forties Charlie*, oil on canvas, 30″ × 24″ (collection Mr Ted Coupland)

North sea oil rig 24″ × 20″ (collection Beecham's Pharmaceuticals)

OPPOSITE PAGE TOP: BP's drilling platform Sea Quest in the Moray Firth Basin. CENTRE: Supply vessel *Edda Sprite* approaching production platform Graythorp 1 in BP's Forties oilfield in the North Sea. BOTTOM: Graythorp 1

followed post-haste. Barbara, back in Cornwall, thought I was indulging in some zany humour when I rang asking her to find my passport!

In my painting life the large industrial scene was already familiar to me. Coal mines of Wales, the massive open-cast china clay mining of Cornwall, commercial working harbours, had all given some insight into large-scale working industry, but the scene of activity a hundred miles offshore from Aberdeen in 1975–76 was truly incredible. Even the very beginning was an indication.

The huge, functional, no-frills helicopter that flew me and some twenty others out, was one of something like thirty flights that day. The Bristow company was operating from Dyce airport what was, at that time, the biggest 'chopper' operation in the world. An hour and a quarter from take-off I watched spellbound from my small window as, dipping, banking and hovering, like some man-made dragon-fly, we descended towards the landing pad of Alpha Bravo. Beside us a 70 ft high steel girder tower spewed a long jet of white-hot flame from its tip, where excess waste oil was being burnt off.

The sickening smell of burning oil seeped through metallic cracks as we circled. The day (it was early March) was sombre and overcast, but the incandescence of the giant torch illuminated the whole upper area as it if were a summer day. As the yellow-targeted steel deck came up to meet us I experienced a feeling of relief. With the heat, the light and the circling aircraft, I thought no longer of a dragon-fly metaphor but drew the ugly parallel of the moth and the candle.

It had been emphasized that I was something of a privileged person. Not exactly a V.I.P., but certainly being offered an experience that many V.I.P.'s were denied at that time. Everybody apparently from the media to junior ministers wanted to observe, at close hand, this latest venture that was to tap one of the richest marine oil fields in the Northern Hemisphere. The hundreds of millions of pounds of state money involved in building some of the biggest oil production platforms, inevitably became headline news. But the emphasis from the P.M. down was to get 'on stream'. There had been enough delays with the fierce unpredictable North Sea storms, and time was of the essence. No one was wanted on the platforms unless they were contributing. The men had no time for sightseers of any rank and the lowest roustabout was far more important than any visiting dignitary. The platform boss or manager, like the captain of a ship (which he often was) had total authority. He could refuse anyone access to his command – and did.

Luckily I had a personal entrée from David Steel, B.P.'s chairman, but even that had been the subject of telex confirmation from platform to shore before I was given my valuable 'pass'. I realized that I had to 'tiptoe thro' the tulips'. The management staff on board could not, understandably, equate the priority I had been given with the seemingly negative qualities I had to offer. Furthermore, for security's sake I had to be allotted a 'minder' and it was difficult to find any man whose duties permitted him to play nursemaid to an itinerant artist. However, they did. For the first few days I behaved humbly, kept my head down, kept out of workers' ways and just observed. I think that when it was realized I was not a total moron, that I didn't want work or men suspended in space and time for me to record like a formal portrait, they started to relax.

I had always had a good head for heights, which also helped. The various working deck levels of these platforms were between 180 and 220 feet above the mean sea level and at that stage of the whole operation, when the 'jackets' (platform skeleton structure) were still in a very basic stage, one was made constantly aware that the angry sea was waiting for a brief misjudgement or slip of the foot. So vertigo was not a malady to be tolerated either. You wore a life-jacket, but if you survived the impact of the fall from that height the sub-zero water temperature gave you perhaps five minutes before hypothermia set in.

I took up sleeping quarters on the crane barge *Hercules* and each waking day was an onslaught of new experiences. Smaller helicopters based 'in the field' operated a shuttle service between the four

*Working Deck of the Cranebarge
Hercules,* oil on canvas 36″ × 48″
(collection Brown and Roote
International)

great platforms, the crane barges and the supply vessels, and I now
had *carte blanche* to hop a shuttle and investigate whatever new scene
was being enacted. The only place I didn't go was down to the sea-
bed with the diving teams, but I did view their hazardous opera-
tions 50 fathoms deep via the closed circuit underwater television,
and talked to the divers as they relaxed, ate and made notes in the
claustrophobic surrounds of their decompression chamber.

It was such a colossal affair – a mammoth meeting of men,
machine and nature in the raw – that a whole book could have been
written about it.

One vivid picture which stays in my memory I think personifies
it all. From the deck of the *Hercules* I watched the second biggest
floating crane in the world (No. 1 of the three fitted to *Hercules*) lift
an eighty-foot long module from the deck of the supply vessel. The
working deck of the crane-barge was virtually at water level. The
crane-deck was perhaps 20 feet higher, but the towering crane jib
itself could reach the furthest main deck of the platform it was
anchored beside. B.P.'s own satellite weather station had told us
that operating conditions were becoming critical. Decisions were
made and lifting began. The 80 by 10 foot square module was to be
one of the important engineering central sections of the platform
and needed to be installed yesterday.

So they proceeded. I watched absolutely awestruck. The cargo

FROM JOHN COLLINS

During that very exciting time in the early 70s of developing Forties, the UK's first major oilfield, Ben Maile was introduced to the few of us involved as a latter day Turner with an interest in industrial archaeology. How this interest was to be compatible with an industry in the forefront of the development of offshore oil technology was initially unclear! However on getting to know Ben, his charming wife Barbara and his paintings at his home in Cornwall, it was plain that here was an artist who was equally at home in the air or at sea as he was on land. As the Forties project combined all three elements, lying 110 miles from Aberdeen at more than an hour's flight by helicopter into the North Sea, we who were to commission him knew we had found the right man.

Ben's appreciation of the tangibles of the environment extended to the abstract of sheer endeavour that North Sea oil development expressed in all its aspects. Here was technology being applied in an unknown environment. At a more human level it meant that even transferring from supply boat to construction barge in a heavy sea became, at times, indescribably difficult.

Ben captured the efforts in a number of superb paintings which are now hung in many parts of the world including both the B.P. and Brown & Root offices in London and Houston. To those of us who were part of the small team involved in Forties, to look at these paintings today is to be immediately transported to those early, heady days of the North Sea oil with its massive and fascinating engineering suport.

For those of us who suffered the birth pangs of Forties, and who saw the tremendous fight against the clock, Ben captured the paradox of isolation yet contact with a base far away. He encapsulated the triumph of emplacing four giant platforms in a hostile sea to produce a total of 600,000 barrels of oil each day. Ben is a friend whose company we enjoy and whose paintings we collect to celebrate a common profound experience.

Away from the oil of our world and the oils of his, Ben and Barabara not only have a great interest but are actively engaged in many charitable works particularly for the aged and the infirm. Their modesty is commendable and their achievements considerable – for this we salute them.

MR. JOHN COLLINS
of Brown & Root (U.K.) Ltd;
and Consultant to The International
Oil Consortium.

Stormswept Forties Alpha, oil on canvas, 30″ × 20″

87

weighed perhaps 600 tonnes – that was no problem – *Hercules* could lift just short of 2,000 tonnes deadweight. The problem was the wind velocity. Accurately predicted by the weatherman, it arrived, when minor snags had delayed the module's arrival at its location a hundred feet above us. Even with the mightiest crane in the world, with computer controls and electronic judgement, when a whacking great metal box is being lowered into position by the crane hook, puny man's physical being is still needed. There still need to be ropes hanging from the box with men on the end of them, teasing and coaxing the contrary swinging monster into position. They had done it before and we had seen them do it, but this time the wind, for an eternity of minutes, played games with them. The great box swung around like a matchbox suspended by a Meccano toy and the men were midget ants. The midgets and the Meccano toy won the day and the job was done, but it was a sobering education for the observer.

Like other painting commissions, the Forties Field had given me great excitement and opened up a totally new area of painting, but more than that, it left me with a sense of great privilege and humility. The sense of privilege was not due to being selected to visit such a high priority field. Not the flattery of V.I.P. treatment, but the privilege I felt in living and doing my work among such a breed of men and being, eventually, accepted among them for however brief a time. The humility, it goes without saying, was in being brought face to face with nature at its most capricious, its most beautiful and its most awesome.

I little thought that I was to experience the same emotions again and in a similar environment, but I did, and if any one scene could vie with the Forties Field for such an experience it could only be the frozen ice-fields of Alaska.

Alaska

B.P.'s own film company had produced a very impressive documentary about the beginnings of their work on the gigantic oil pipeline in Alaska. Had it been produced within the highly competitive television industry it would have captured all awards on offer. Its effect upon me was such that Sir David Steel, B.P.'s Chairman, obviously aware that my painter's antennae were highly receptive to such a scene, offered me the rare prize of experiencing it first hand.

"Would you like to go over and do for us there what you did in the Forties Field?" Would I! I thanked my lucky stars that my professional effort on that former commission had been successful enough to make this offer possible. My spell in the North Sea had been a remarkable sojourn, with its immense concept of engineering. It was a great challenge to any painter although its marine setting gave me a favoured and familiar background for everything I produced there. Alaska was for me a totally alien field. I had always been a sun worshipper and though Jack London had provided favourite reading matter in years gone by, the thought of

The Haul Road near the Brooks Range

a spell in such zero arctic climes did cause a few misgivings. However they were outweighed, as ever, by my insatiable curiosity aroused by that brilliant camera team.

The film had borne an odd contradictory title *The End of the Road*. The colossal feat of building an 800-mile pipeline across the frozen north was only just beginning. Before any start could be made the long 'haul road' had to be constructed, the road upon which all the equipment and supplies were to be trucked in. The road had to end before the pipeline could begin – hence the title.

A fter a novel polar flight from Heathrow, London, to Anchorage, Alaska, I was impatient to get up to the north slope where it was all happening, but I had to kick my heels for a few days. There were mundane things to be done. I had to be kitted out for a start and when I was measured up for a fur-lined parka, long woollen socks, and iceboots, I began to realise that I really was heading for Jack London country!

There was education, too, rules and regulations to be acquainted with, survival laws and priority systems. Despite the arctic clothing there was an air of unreality about it. The overnight growth of Anchorage had produced its modern, highrise hotels and despite the snow around there was a highly cultured social scene that

The Alaska Pipeline

89

The Haul Road leaving Thompson Pass

FROM JACK BIRKS

As I write this I am looking at one of Ben Maile's paintings of a section of the most northerly part of the Alaskan Pipeline in a wasteland of frozen tundra. This brought back recollections of our visit together in 1976 travelling the whole of the 800 miles length of the pipeline route from the Prudhoe Bay Oilfield on the north slope of Alaska to the oil terminal at Valdez in Prince William Sound. A new world for both the oil engineer and the artist.

Seeing the construction of the first major oil field in Alaska was a rare and exciting experience particularly when seen through the eyes of the artist.

The Prudhoe Bay Oilfield was discovered in 1968 being the largest oilfield ever discovered in the whole of North America. The site of the oilfield is only some two miles from the Arctic Ocean where land and sea are virtually indistinguishable from each other being frozen and snow-covered for most of the year with temperatures as low as minus 60 degrees Fahrenheit. However, during the short six weeks of summer when there is permanent daylight the countryside bursts into colour.

The route of the pipeline sounds like a story from goldrush days running south from Prudhoe Bay across the flat tundra to the Brooks Mountain Range, crossing the Atigun Pass at a height of 4800 feet and then plunging down through mountains, streams and valleys to the Ukon River, then on through hilly country bypassing the town of Fairbanks, climbing over the Alaskan mountain range through the Copper River Basin and finally over the last major obstacle at Thomson Pass down to the Valdez Terminal.

For the first 400 miles or so the 48 inch diameter pipeline is raised above ground level on specially designed H supports to prevent the hot oil melting the frozen permafrost. South of the Ukon River the pipeline is buried to a depth of about 6 feet for the remaining 400 miles to Valdez. Although the whole of the pipeline had been delivered to Alaska by 1971, construction was delayed for three years due to environmental concern for the protection of the very sensitive Arctic environment. However, in 1974 the first phase of construction started by building 360 miles of access roads to the pipeline from the Ukon River to the Prudhoe Bay Oilfield. In total there were 31 construction camps along the pipeline route with a workforce of over 20,000 men and women involved, twelve pumping stations along the pipeline together with pipeline crossings of some 600 rivers and streams including a 2300 feet two lane bridge crossing the Ukon river, making this the most outstanding pipeline project of all time. Costs were equally outstanding of some $10 million per mile of line.

His paintings for me capture the magnificence of the engineering effort in that beautiful and remote Arctic land.

New oilfields are now being developed near to Prudhoe Bay adding to the 2 million barrels of oil each day flowing down the pipeline to Valdez which will remain for many years the largest single source of American oil supplies.

DR JACK BIRKS
Chairman, Charterhouse Oil Inc.
(Late Deputy Chairman, B.P.)

90

The Haul Road, oil on canvas, 30″ × 48″ (collection British Petroleum)

embraced me, so that my impending destination seemed more of a story-book world than actual fact waiting just around the corner. In reality it was not just around the corner. It was a three-hour flight away over the mountainous Brooks range and through Thompson Pass. At Thompson the plane turned left when 'Old Snowy' came up to starboard, and we started descending until the 300-foot-high pine forests came into view. We slipped over the top of the pine trees and made a stomach churning landing at Crazy Horse.

I got to know this procedure pretty well, after having to attempt three flights out from Anchorage in the little twin-engined Piper Cherokee. On the first attempt Anchorage's sophistication disappeared at the airfield when a blizzard swept in and frozen snow

Snow Drift at Nabors Rig, oil on
canvas, 24″ × 36″ (collection
British Petroleum)

clung to our wingtips all the way over the Brooks range and
eventually getting so thick that we had to abort and return to base.

The next morning when we set off there was only light snow –
no blizzard, and we made it to Thompson Pass – but there the snow
thickened and at 7000 feet we couldn't find 'Old Snowy', a massive
overhanging glacial bluff that the bush pilots used as a sign-post –
so we aborted again. The third time we made it and I found that the
romantically named Crazy Horse was a 400-yard clearing hacked
out of the forest and the landing strip marked with 40-gallon oil-
drums. The little Piper aircraft skidded along the frozen runway
surface in a series of yawing slides before coming to a halt with
maybe 50 yards to spare. The pilot then gunned one engine and
kicked the opposite rudder so that we swung back into the direction
we had landed and taxied back to the very rudimentary control
tower and small reception office.

"Everybody ashore," jocularly called out our pilot. It was
obviously quite a normal, routine flight. Nothing untoward, and
blizzards and 'Old Snowy' permitting he would continue to repeat
it for a long time to come. All five of us heaved our luggage out of

the Piper Cherokee and plodded ashore; one replacement Met Officer, three engineers and the itinerant painter. We were visiting No. 6 pumping station, situated some 80 miles east of Fairbanks, and one of the very important staging posts and transfer stations. When completed it would form a vital part of the 800-mile-long pipeline that ran south from Prudhoe Bay up in the Arctic Circle to Valdes, ranging across frozen tundra, over rivers, and under them, crossing mountain ranges and redwood forests on the way.

By strange contrast the flight up to Prudhoe itself, 300 miles inside the Arctic Circle where temperatures then, at the end of winter, were 35–40 degrees below, was quite sophisticated. Boeing Jets of Polarair Services were making regular flights and coming to a halt a stone's throw away from the front door of the airport reception. There were no height problems with these aircraft, no Thompson Pass to manoeuvre, no 'Old Snowy' to consult and no hacked out strips in a surrounding forest to land on. At Prudhoe as far as the eye could see, was a vast, flat, frozen waste. They had put down runway markers and windsocks but the pilot never needed to overshoot, he couldn't run out of landing space however much he

Laying the Pipeline, oil on canvas, 28″ × 36″ (collection British Petroleum)

93

tried. I had earlier seen the B.P. television documentary and so had some anticipation of what was to come. But the visual effect of such a vast frozen terrain was mind-blowing.

The Nabors rig, the first to pump oil up from below the frozen Arctic sea, was a jumbo sized installation by any standards, yet the endless ridges of frozen waves extending as far as the eye could see somehow reduced its scale. Distances, heights, all could be quite deceptive. In the brilliant clear air it was easy to assume that a distant building or installation was a mere five-minute walk away, when in fact it was a five-mile truck ride. Not that you would have walked anyway, walking was kept to a minimum. Breathing in air that reminded me of mountain ozone and wearing sunglasses to combat snowglare from a gorgeous sun, it was easy to forget that the temperature was at least 30 degrees below freezing point. The lightweight, but highly effective nylon and fur-lined protective clothing kept at bay the ever-waiting hazard of hypothermia. A brisk walk was often a temptation and eventually with experience and guidance I did walk, though there were rules of caution and commonsense to observe.

There had been a case of a worker who was fit, young and adequately clothèd, who had completed a shift of strenuous work, had scorned the transport back to his hut, walked a brisk couple of miles or so then stopped to have a smoke and a rest. He was resting totally when they found him eight hours later. It was not the walking that was the fatal error but the stopping to rest which allowed layers of moist condensation built up by his own body heat between his clothes to quickly freeze when the movement and circulation slowed and stopped. Inside his protective jacket and nylon sheathed overtrousers every other layer of clothing had turned to ice. They had told me this story on my arrival. They told it to all newcomers as part of their safety briefing but it took a few milder experiences for this warning to sink in.

Deception was everywhere. Early one day I was clambering over some pipework to find a slight drop the other side, no more than maybe 4 to 5 feet. The sloping drop had frozen to a small glacial effect and I slid easily down it. At the bottom, attractive rounded crests of soft snow had formed from a short wind flurry an hour or two earlier, and as I slipped to the bottom I put out a gloved hand to steady myself. Ouch! the soft mounds of snow were like solid concrete. It had frozen as it fell with no booted feet or truck wheels passing that way to flatten it. One thing about the cold was that it reduced the feeling of pain and when I removed my glove the knuckles were visibly swelling with a ripe shade of blue. But, despite the deceptions, the hazards and the unbelievable cold, it captured my imagination as much as anywhere I had been.

Even now the memories are mixed, but still vivid. For instance the parking lot filled with trucks, trailers, crawlers and cars. The working shift finished, drivers gone and each and every engine running at fast idling revs I knew they would continue to run night and day, working or parked until the vehicle was scrapped. Out there if an engine is switched off for more than three minutes it

Snow drifts on the Pipeline

OPPOSITE: *Close up, the Pipeline*, oil on canvas, 30″ × 20″ (collection British Petroleum)

95

Snowclearing at Valdez, oil on canvas, 24″ × 36″ (Artist's collection)

freezes up solid and never runs again. It is vitally important that fuel tanks are filled up when they finish work for the day.

The memory is still with me of that great pipeline, 4 foot diameter, supported on massive pillars six foot above the ground running across the tundra as far as the eye could see. Actually traversing a straight line, yet every 60 feet or so 'kinked' to allow for expansion and contraction movement caused by the heat of the oil inside and the variation of temperature outside. I remember the hectic working scene, tractors, trucks, cranes, pipes and men. Time midnight, but as light as day under the great sodium flares and then a minute later the whole event 'whited out' by a freezing, blinding snow blizzard that screamed down from nowhere.

I recall the giant snow-ploughs and tractors the next morning clearing the ten foot drifts left by the blizzard, of getting out of the four wheel drive truck on the banks of the Yukon River, and walking across its snow covered frozen waters, with a sky and sun above that would have seemed normal in the Mediterranean. At Prudhoe itself a mile out from the shore line, tankers, motorised barges and tugs lay up to their plimsole lines in ice. Solid ice that reached down 40 feet before the water flowed freely. They were the ones that 3 months earlier had made the last desperate try to deliver, disembark and return as the creeping freeze-up of winter had suddenly accelerated upon them.

A memorable country indeed, and one more that I vowed I would return to one day.

Thames Flood Barrier

Nearly every time I made my way down to Greenwich Reach to the site of the Flood Barrier it was hard to disassociate it from the sombre, muddy, but languid movements of the River Thames. Over the period of some 6 months or so of my visits with sketch-book and camera, the weather, surprisingly, was reasonably mild. There were downpours of rain, but no threatening activity on Old Father Thames's part, that suggested this whole massive engineering concept was a security undertaking of the first order.

The Flood Barrier was designed and built to save many square miles of land and property – not to mention human lives. Even the shipping that came through while I was there did not seem, in those calm waters, to have a credible connection with maritime activity. Little coasting vessels chugged up from down river. Tankers from

The Thames Flood Barrier under construction

TOP: *Hydraulic control bay*, oil on canvas, 28″ × 38″

ABOVE: *Dredging*, oil on canvas, 24″ × 36″

my old friends of B.P. crawled past, as if they never thought of putting to sea, and the busiest activity was the work-boats, taking the workers from one side of the river to the other.

It was not until a certain day in March, that a force 7 took hold of the Thames at the Medway and roared violently up river. It was just an average high spring tide, but with the forces of nature all harnessed together with the worst intent I realised for the first time just what an enormously high tide could achieve under freak conditions.

Central Pier under construction, oil on canvas 30″ × 40″

The immensity and strength of those great centre piers no longer presented any question – one day if those conditions did arrive all of their strength and modern technology would be needed.

My first thoughts upon seeing the curved, shell-like domes of the hydraulic stations were that there was a strong Dutch influence, and people seeing my finished paintings often made the same observation. One particular view of the whole span across the river suggests a long line of Dutch windmills with their sails removed. But although there were, I believe, some Dutch and German

Like Sail-less Dutch Windmills, oil on canvas 30" × 48"

companies involved in the dredging, the designers and construction otherwise were all British.

Perhaps battling against the encroachment of water creates a similar outlook to the minds of people who otherwise think quite differently.

Unlike my sojourn in the North Sea with B.P. these structures, even in the early days, never quite suggested the same element of

risk or hazard. It was when the engineers took me into the servicing
shaft that I first felt a little chilling of the spine. This was an 8-foot
diameter steel and concrete tunnel that was being built on the bed of
the river running through the foundation of the barrier. It served to
carry communication lines, power cables and other technical
matters as well as a continual linking of each section to the barrier.
When I walked through to be brought up short by a massive

Giant Cranes at South Bank, oil on canvas, 30″ × 40″

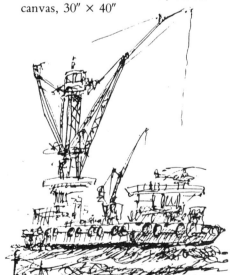

concrete plug (at that point they had got about halfway across) I realised then that I was right at the bottom of Old Father Thames with some 60 feet of his water above me, and in fact millions of gallons surging past, just the other side of that concrete plug. I retracted my steps and made my way to the service station on the bank, realising that from that moment on into time men would be continually traversing that shaft, living and working on the very bed of the river.

Thank goodness I am a painter and only have to view and record those scenes.

Outside of the oil industry, I doubt if any other engineering project has seen the use of so many huge tower cranes on one site. From north to south bank, working from shore, from linking causeways, and sometimes from great barges in mid-river itself, they reared over the barrier 100 feet high and more. Approaching by boat from downstream, particularly when the Thames was wearing an early morning cloak of grey river mist, their skeletal gantries seemed for all the world like some colossal, prehistoric birds, watching vigilantly over their nests.

THE MARY ROSE

ABOVE: HRH Prince Charles with Sir Eric Drake at the presentation of *The Mary Rose, 1545*. OPPOSITE: *The Mary Rose 1545*, oil on canvas, 40″ × 30″ (collection HRH Prince Charles)

It wasn't easy to project on to that mental screen when I first got involved with the *Mary Rose* – the marvellous old Tudor galleon/ warship that went to the bottom in 1545, under the very eyes of King Henry VIII himself.

In 1976, when the recovery team were still working out a scheme to reclaim her and bring her to the surface, I was persuaded by Margaret Rule to help swell the funds needed by using my brush and palette. Paint the *Mary Rose* – as she was 450 years ago – under full sail – a romantic, dramatic picture of her that would appeal to all. A painting that could be reproduced as an expensive Limited Edition print. It seemed a sensible enough scheme. I was well established in the fine art print world. Collectors were usually ready to buy a new Ben Maile Limited Edition, and a subject that was beginning to catch the public attentionn could be a winner. But what did she look like in 1545?

All they had of her on record was an ancient, stylized two-dimensional drawing that in the 16th-century did not necessarily mean that the recording artist had even seen the ship. Artistic licence and verbal description often took the place of actualy seeing the subject in those days. But after a lot of research and consultation with the *Mary Rose* team, my final result did not in fact depart very much from that earlier official record.

When my eventual working colour sketches met the approval of the redoubtable Margaret Rule herself I proceeded to work on the final canvas in oils with total confidence – if Margaret Rule said it was right I had not a thing to worry about!

As I lost myself in the excitement of producing that work, one

FROM MARGARET RULE
In 1976 when I first met Ben Maile, little was known about the real appearance of the *Mary Rose*. Only one artist's impression of the old ship was in existence.

Our limited experience under water since 1971 had done little or nothing to enhance our understanding of the ship. What we had was a wreck lying on her side, entombed in evil smelling mud on the sea bed, with only ⅛th of her upper side exposed to the gloomy Solent waters.

The thought of meeting Ben to discuss the creation of a modern in-formed interpretation of Henry VIII's lost war ship threw me into despair. However the meeting began cordially and warmed as we began to talk; not about the ship, but about the men who built her, sailed her, fought her and died on board in the summer of 1545.

Together we attempted to understand the spirit of that age. How could the six or seven hundred soldiers and sailors, reputed to have been on board when she sank, live and work on board a ship the size of the ferryboat which plies to and fro across the entrance to Portsmouth Harbour?

Ben understood, and met the challenge.

The vision of the gallant ship which emerged from his canvas captured for me the essence of 16th century maritime endeavour. Under Ben's brush my dream took substance . . . a painting for everyone to enjoy and one to reinterpret for himself.

Margaret Rule

MRS. MARGARET RULE C.B.E.
Archaeological Director,
The Mary Rose Trust

strange thought began to evolve. More a feeling than tangible thought. I was the first person to depict the ship since that first artist produced his drawing for the King's naval records. The fact that I was painting – recording something that was still at the bottom of the sea – that I was putting into a visual form something that had perished all that time ago, was slightly, well, uncanny.

That fact gave me a feeling of privilege, but the slow realization that in all that time no other records, illustrations or information had come to light made me sense that I was in a unique position at that moment. It gave me an unusual feeling of responsibility. I was painting a portrait of a ship which had sunk 450 years ago. There was an obligation to that artist who drew her first of all. There was an obligation to the ancient timbered skeleton that one day soon

The Tog Mor, 6 am November 1982, oil on canvas, 40″ × 30″

RIGHT: *Up and Away*, oil on canvas, 30″ × 48″

FROM LORD CALDECOTE

The Artist's brief was to paint a portrait of an old lady, who had died over 400 years previously, and whose remains now lay at the bottom of the Solent, covered in silt and mud.

The Artist was Ben Maile, and the old lady was King Henry VIII's warship, the *Mary Rose*, which had tragically sunk all those years before.

In 1976, still a long way from the actual attempt to recover the ship, the *Mary Rose* Committee were charged with increasing sponsorship and funding.

Among the many industrial and commercial companies who responded to their appeal was the oil giant B.P., who, in their turn, introduced Mr Maile to the Mary Rose Project.

An avid devotee of all things maritime, Ben Maile reacted enthusiastically and after considerable research his romantic impression in oils of the *Mary Rose* in full sail made a splendid project for new fund raising. Reproduced as a signed Limited Edition and launched at London's Mansion House in 1981,

his work on our behalf was well rewarded.

Ben's interest and enthusiasm were maintained, and when eventually it came to the great day of the 'lift' he was the one to whom the Trust turned to depict, with brush and canvas, the scene of the recovery.

Caldecote

THE RT. HON. THE VISCOUNT CALDECOTE, DSC

107

The Bones of the Mary Rose, acrylic sketch

was going to be reverently raised to the surface, and there was an obligation to all those souls who went down with her, so suddenly, so tragically.

Six years later I had become so involved with the whole absorbing saga of the *Mary Rose* that the Trust asked me to be present on the great day of the intended recovery. By this time I bore the proud title of officially appointed artist to the Mary Rose Trust – a title that gave me greater pleasure than any I gained in the past in the art world.

With the recovery, in October 1982, the accent was on 20th-century technology rather than 16th-century history. With the giant floating crane, Tog Mor, the massive lifting cradle designed by computers, with technicians monitoring control of the operation on television, the scene was somewhat reminiscent of my days in the North Sea with BP.

The following year, when my canvases and drawings of this epic occasion went on exhibition, there was another painting in complete contrast to all the others: *The Sinking of the Mary Rose*. This, the painting that should have been done first, was the very last I did.

A back-to-front process, maybe, but I had needed all those years of involvement of seeing her contents and treasures brought to the surface. I had needed all that time to find out about the *Mary Rose* and about those who sailed in and sank with her. When she finally came back again – back to Portsmouth – it was like a ghost being laid. Thanks to Margaret Rule and her team of divers, I knew how she really had looked that day and just how she had sunk and where. And when I painted this final picture I was filling a gap that had been left blank all that time.

OPPOSITE: *High and Dry*, oil on canvas, 36″ × 28″ (collection Mr E. Jamieson)

FROM MALCOLM COCKELL

It has been said to me that *The Sinking of the Mary Rose* is a sad and tragic painting and that is very true. The event depicted here, which took place some 435 years ago, I would describe as being strange. It now affects the lives of many people who were involved with the recovery of the artefacts and the ship; it is quite probable that the impact today is even greater than of that of the disaster at the time.

During the recovery of the ship on the 10/11th October 1982, there was an occasion which was particularly significant to me; during an operation to overcome a problem, part of the ship's structure was revealed above the surface of the sea when only a few people were present, at 4.00 a.m. The sea was dead calm and only the moon lit the scene. We could almost touch the timbers and in this atmosphere the souls of some 700 men seemed to be reaching out across the centuries to communicate with us. It was another 24 hours before the recovery was completed and even then only after a number of problems had been resolved. One had the impression that the sea and the vessel, which had lain undisturbed for so long, were not going to give up their treasures easily.

Ben's painting captures this mood and displays the disastrous sinking with so much action that you can almost hear the panic.

It is a constant reminder that many of us, in diverse ways, even today, have had our fortunes and destinies touched by an event which took place such a long time ago; we must always be respectful of this. Which events that have taken place recently will have the same effect on the lives of people in a few hundred years time? The actual occurrence can pass so quickly that we are not always aware of the relevance and significance at that moment.

I feel, therefore, very privileged to have been involved in the recovery and, I believe Ben, for his part, shares this sentiment.

MR M. W. COCKELL
Manager, Babcock Power Limited,
Construction Division, Tipton.

The Sinking of the Mary Rose, oil on canvas, 30″ × 48″ (collection Mr Malcolm Cockell)

The Limited Edition presentation on board *SS Canberra* with Mrs Margaret Rule, CBE and Captain Bob Ellingham

In 1545 King Henry VIII watched 'the flower of his fleet' struggle and die.

In 1984 Margaret Rule, who had masterminded the Tudor ship's recovery, joined me in presenting to the SS *Canberra*, P.&O.'s giant cruise liner, a picture of the *Mary Rose* sinking (like many in city commerce, P.&O. had been one of the early sponsors of the project).

The picture was No. 1 of the Limited Edition from my oil painting entitled with that sombre name.

Knowing of seamen's inbuilt superstition of all things connected with the sea, I had been a little concerned about presenting them with a picture depicting the finality dreaded by all seafarers. However, my fears were groundless. Not long before, the *Canberra* had survived, nobly, all the fearful hazards of the Falklands campaign, and where Exocet missiles had failed, they obviously had little fear of superstitious omens.

At the formal handover jovial Captain Bob Ellingham quoted to me P.&O.'s headline to their press handout of the occasion. 'P.&O.'s flagship, *SS Canberra,* salutes the flagship of King Henry VIII.'

Now when I board the great liner, better known to her 'regulars', affectionately, as 'the great white whale', that picture of the *Mary Rose* sinking, greets me. Resplendently mounted and framed it holds a proud position on the mahogany wall of the main vestibule lounge on 'A' deck. Surrounded by plaques, prints and various commemorative inscriptions presented from all over the world, the picture does not over-emphasise the tragedy – in that company it merely substantiates what a timeless, continuing history of events is shared by all those who go down to the sea in ships.

THE CORNISH
IN AMERICA

Cornish Miners
in America

It was on an early trip to America, 1971/72 I think, that I first saw Virginia City. The town was a fascinating living museum, re-living an age of 100 years before. Clapboarded hotels, saloons and houses of doubtful repute, all with their outside board-walks and hitching rails. It was more realistic than many a Hollywood film set, and when my hosts took me up to see the towns 'Boothill' I was prepared to see something equally impressive even though I mentally queried their taste. Surely, reconstructing a graveyard was over-gilding the lily? Shock followed suspicion. The graveyard was certainly authentic looking, and the Italian marble headstones (markers, the Americans called them, with unashamed directness) surely could not have been a secondary planting.

No. This Boothill had to be, as my hosts assured me, the genuine article. I bent over the markers morbidly interested in the names of long ago citizens who died with their boots on. Second and intriguing shock. The graveyard abounded with Cornish names. Only those who are Celtic or have deep affinity with the Royal Duchy can know what emotion can be aroused by seeing the unmistakable Tremaynes, Pascoes and Penroses on a dry, dusty hill-top, 6,000 miles away from their native shores. I searched further and found a veritable colony of Cornish names, Mitchell, Trethewey, Pearce and Bawden. The questions saturated my mind and bewildered my polite and hospitable American friends. The first lead I had was when it was suggested they could have been there because of silver or gold. Nearby, running like a twisting, underground river, ran the famous Colmstock lode. Those Cornishmen had been there because they were miners. Years before I had sketched and painted in oil, tall stacked engine houses, that spike the skyline right through the middle of my adopted country. They had been dramatic, visual subjects, that were an ideal inspiration for painter or poet. But whilst I had scribbled poor verse about them and recreated them in oils and water-colour, I had not, to my shame, gone beyond the façade and dipped deeper into their history. Now with an intriguing link to their human partners the incentive was upon me to know more.

Over the years I read and visited museums and libraries, talking to old timers, whose memories could still stretch back to fathers and uncles who had worked the mines. I learned of tributemen and tut workers, of boys, ten years old, who carried the tallows 1000 feet and more underground, of whims and lodes and levels, of winding engines and man engines and captains and adventurers. A vast industry in copper and tin that kept 100,000 Cornish families if not in comfort then in work. Its industry held all the dramas, tragedies, the romancés and comedy to a degree whereby, had Cornwall then had its own Charlotte Bronte, Blackmoor or Hardy, we would still be reading tales that might have paled the dark satanic mills of the North into insignificance.

With newly acquired knowledge I now, on every subsequent trip to America, take time out to trace evidence of the Cornish Miners' emigration to the States in the middle and late 19th-century.

Emigration broadsheet issued in Padstow in 1844. This brig was probably engaged in the American timber trade and carried emigrants on the return voyages as 'paying ballast'.

Boothill, Virginia City, where it all started

When the Cornish Tin Mining suffered massive collapse then the Cornishmen took their skills with them to a new world that appeared to be inundated with every mineral known to man. The trouble was, the valuable minerals were deep down and still being mined by incredibly primitive methods. The Cornishman, or 'Cousin Jack' as he became known, was the finest 'deep hardrock' miner in the Western hemisphere and America welcomed him with open arms. From lead to iron and silver to gold, mines flourished and died, as new ones were discovered over every other hill, river or desert. Cornishmen came, brought their families, settled or married other immigrants, and started new families.

Eventually the massive strikes faded, even in this land of plenty. The hysteria and gold fever ran its course and by the time an itinerant English painter came on the scene all that was left was history. However this had been carefully filed and documented by those same Cornish families and their descendants. The excitement of discovering second generation 'Cousin Jacks' never failed me whether the discovery was made in sunny California, frozen Alaska, Wisconsin or Arizona.

In 1980, I had produced enough irrefutable evidence and badgered some friends down at B.B.C.'s South Western region, enough to persuade them to agree to a documentary on the theme 'The Cornish Miner in America'.

On the 17th March 1982, I flew out to Madison, Wisconsin U.S.A, for the start of a 'reconnaissance' trip in preparation for the actual film production exercise. Over the years the basic plot of the story we were to produce had formed very tangibly in my mind. I had a fat collection of outline notes, historic references and long lists of contacts and places spread right across the States. With a producer and production team I had got to know well on previous programmes, we had a provisional scenario worked out. My job now was to do a 'dummy' run for the programme, confirm locations and subjects, eliminate any that might seem suspect, investigate new ones, as yet untapped, and finally arrive at a firm

FROM SUE LAWLEY
Success and modesty are not unnatural partners, but they do seem to be rare ones. Ben Maile is that rare human being – successful and modest.

I first met him in the early seventies when I was a freelance reporter for BBC Plymouth. Ben was my 'assignment'. My editor wanted a film portrait of this artist who had tucked himself away in a corner of Cornwall and was steadily becoming a national name.

My sister loves painting so I had taken her along too. The film was a long day in the making – not least because Ben and Jane, my sister, got into deep conversation at the easel as we set up the camera . . . and by the time we were ready to shoot he was halfway through a lesson on the technique of oils which couldn't be interrupted. That's typical Ben. He's not only modest, but a passionate enthusiast who wants the world to share his enthusiasm.

He also has another force in his life. She's called Barbara, his business manager, his chief critic, and his wife. It was Barbara, who steered us diplomatically through that first day with an awareness of everyone's professional requirements and it's been Barbara who's been our social secretary ever since!

She once told me a secret. Ben has painted a portrait of me . . . as I once appeared some years ago on the cover of the *Radio Times* in a romantic Ascot hat! Will it be the climax of a beautiful friendship, the day he lets me see it? Or will the natural honesty of the artist refuse to flatter me one bit! I hope it'll be the latter – and I'm sure it won't make a scrap of difference to my friendship with Ben.

Sue Lawley

MISS SUE LAWLEY
BBC Television. *Nationwide, Tonight* and *Six O'Clock News*

115

Cornish 'Cousin Jacks' at the Empire Mine, Grass Valley, California

FROM TED COUPLAND

I first met Ben Maile about 15 years ago. I found Ben in the old studio in Newquay and we talked for an hour or so about his paintings. This was the first time that I had seen Ben's work and my name was immediately added to his followers.

I bought two paintings, both quite large, one of which was of an old Cornish Tin Mine and the other was of the China Clay Works at St. Austell. I insisted that I took the paintings home with me and they just fitted in my car. The only way in which this could be done was for my friend to drive, myself in the back with the paintings resting on the front passengers seat and the frame under my chin. If there had been any sudden braking I would have lost my head as effectively as Charles 1st!

Since those days I have gradually added to my collection. In the main these are paintings of places, not all of which I had been to at the time of buying the pictures, but I am up to date with the exception of one. This is a recent acquisition and is a painting of Virginia City and is part of a series which Ben painted, this, no doubt mentioned elsewhere in the book. I have a great deal of fun explaining to people the connection between a painting of Virginia City and my first painting of an old Cornish Tin Mine. This is in no way apparent. An exception to works of places is a magnificent painting of a North Sea Oil Rig, which I look at constantly. I am fascinated by the wind whipping off the top of the waves and an area of the sea which is dark, deep and frightening; the whole painting is full of atmosphere. I have no desire to be on an oil rig in such weather conditions. The painting next to it is of the Grand Canal in Venice, which I know very well. I can look into this for several minutes and almost feel the heat from a very hot day. One of the great things about Ben's paintings, to me at least, is that no matter how long I have had some of them I still get great pleasure in looking at them, getting lost in the subject. I can feel that I am there.

Another painting of Ben's which I much regret not owning is a painting of St. Paul's, and I am ashamed of the reason. The painting was of the Cathedral on a grey winters day, the lower half was shrouded in mist with red London Transport buses just shewing through, the upper half in brighter light and more detail. I thought the cupola on the top of the dome was higher than I remembered it and consequently I did not buy the painting. On checking up, I found Ben to be right and I was wrong. However, I am sure that a street scene I have of Innsbruck shows a sign of the left-hand side which belongs to the Adler Hotel around the corner! I'm probably wrong again, nevertheless it is good fun trying to work out exactly where Ben stood when making his sketches. I have a painting of the San Francisco waterfront and I think Ben must have got into the U.S. Navy establishment on the other side of the bay but I have never got around to asking him.

You will have gathered by now that owning a few Ben Maile paintings has given me an enormous amount of pleasure, and I am certain that other collectors feel the same way. I made up my mind a long time ago to stop buying because I told myself I had enough, and they were getting too expensive, but that was six paintings ago and I have just discovered another wall in the house which would take another!

MR. TED COUPLAND
Principal,
Thameside Construction Company

Virginia City, Nevada, oil on canvas, 24″ × 36″ (collection Mr Ted Coupland)

itinerary that would enable us, over some four weeks, to put sufficient film into the can to produce two 30 minute documentaries plus four 5 minute spots for local regional use. I knew by now that there was enough material in the existing history of this epic to produce a documentary every week for a year, without repetition or risk of boredom. So the question was, where to apply the stops? What to leave out?

At Wisconsin this decision was made no easier. The lead mines of Mineral Point and Plattville had given the early immigrant Cornishmen not only their first taste of mining in the New World, but had also taken them into the Indian Wars of 1840/50. There were magic names such as *Chief Black Hawk* and the *Chippeuas,* the *Winnebagos* and *Colonel Dodge,* of Dodge City fame, real 'Boys Own' paper stuff.

My dear friends Al and Edna Moyle, members of the Madison State Historical Society, not only supplied me with much valued information, but gave me treasured contacts to follow up right across the country. As second generation Cornishmen they were typical of many we were to meet on the whole memorable trip. They had all the outgoing generous hospitality of the American, but also possessed the fiercely loyal pride of their Cornish blood.

In March, Wisconsin has a cold climate. Lake Mendota was still frozen over, and the old hill mines of Mineral Point were covered in snow; but my next stop at Duluth, on the frozen shores of Lake

117

TOP: A disused mining shack near De Soto, Arizona. CENTRE: Frank Matthews visiting the old Levant Mine in Cornwall. ABOVE: Old chuck wagon at Sovereign Hill, Nevada

RIGHT: *The Wagon Train*, oil on canvas, 28″ × 36″ (Artist's collection)

Superior was colder still. The Cornish links there were not as pronounced as further east in North Michigan. I rented a car and drove approximately 500 miles along the great highway that runs almost parallel to the Canadian border, heading for the upper Michigan Peninsular. With every mile it got colder and by the time I reached the small township of Negaunee I thanked my lucky stars

Vulture Mine, Arizona, oil on canvas 30″ × 40″

The Cleator Hotel, oil on canvas 28″ × 36″

that I had thought to pack some of the winter clothing I had worn in Alaska. Negaunee, however, was worth any amount of discomfort to find the rich and rewarding personalities such as the grand old man Frank Matthews, who was eventually to become the veritable star of our small film. From here I drove south again back to Madison City to rest briefly and dine with Al and Edna Moyle, before flying south to Phoenix, Arizona.

After Michigan's sub zero temperatures the change to the 80 plus heat of Arizona was daunting. But there were places with names like *Tombstone, Globe, Pearce* and *Galena* to explore. All mining towns, ghost towns for the most part, but all with a wealth of Cornish history. And the drive up the mountain highway through the Bradshaws to Prescott, 5,000 feet, took me into beautifully crisp cool air again, yet with a cloudless sun. There more old mining towns, such as *Jerome,* still lived in with its strong Cornish contingent, and the mountains and valleys for miles around hid within their dusty folds, a happy hunting ground of prospectors' dreams. *Vulture Mine, De Soto, Crown King, Cleator,* and many more, which were just a tumble of rotting timbers and flooded shafts.

On high ground in the dry atmosphere old prospectors' shacks still stood, decaying slowly, corrugated roofs reflecting a fierce sun, and their shadows hiding rattle snakes, scorpions and monstrous spiders. But all around was a magnificent landscape, and the day I stood on a narrow mountain track 7,000 feet up and looked *down* on a beautiful giant golden eagle, was as great a thrill as any. He was climbing easily, in wide spirals on a thermal from the lush green valley below and I speculated upon how the 'Cousin Jacks' might

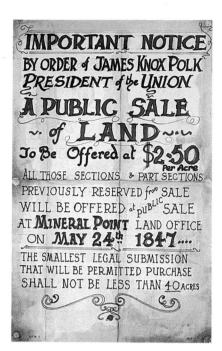

Public Land Sale Notice, Mineral Point

have responded to this great country. With their love of individual freedom, and the memory of their spacious Cornish moors, and lofty coastline, this other open spacious landscape must have been a great consolation.

But the itinerary – or its completion – called, and time was running out.

I discovered Violet Thomas, a second cousin to my own Cornish wife, living in Prescott, and she undertook to organise the whole of our production trip in that area on our return (and she did). I drove back to Phoenix City – how glossy and artificial it seemed after the genuine, forthright characters I had encountered up there in the mountains – and I booked on the next flight out to California to explore, once again, the very first gold rush country.

In North California, on the other side of the Sierra Nevadas just below Lake Donner, was the little township of Grass Valley. I knew that it was probably the largest Cornish contingent in the whole of America. I had flown into San Francisco, to be met with floods, drove out to meet ice and snow up in the Sierras and after being snow bound in Auburn for a day eventually slithered over ice roads into Grass Valley. The marvellous welcome I had there included the promise of staging a 'Cornish Christmas' for the benefit of the cameras when we arrived the following month. This was already pressing us close, and having been flood bound in San Francisco, snow bound in the Sierras and toasted in the Arizona desert, I arrived home 23,000 miles and fifteen days later, still bemused from jet lag, but with a very firm if basic itinerary and very excited at the prospects created.

That was a Saturday. After a day's meeting and talks with producer and director on the Monday, we met up at Heathrow on Wednesday to fly out again, to at last do the job that I had dreamed about for so long.

Working the Stope, oil on canvas, 30″ × 40″

OPPOSITE: *Frank Matthews, GOM*, oil on canvas, 36″ × 28″

FROM DAVID WAY

Mystery and romance was the legend – and it was never more than a legend that the miners of Cornwall left behind in their old engine houses.

But in the United States it's the tradition of the adventurer, the pioneer, and the buccaneer that marks the ghost towns which straddle the States from the borders of Mexico to the edge of the Great Lakes.

The townships once roared with activity as the Cornish hunted any kind of ore that was reported in hard rock. Now some have sadly, almost squalidly fallen to the desert heat, others are tourist traps in the pocket of 'improvers' with fruit machines, providing the only adventure. Others, though, are genuine enough with one man doubling up as Town Mayor, grizzled bar tender, and leg pulling guide presiding over cobwebbed beer pumps and faded maps of the old railroads. Reminders of the schools, the churches, the shops and the mines when ore was shipped out by the hundred ton. Now, its all old men's tales.

But the galvanised Cornish – those sons and daughters of the original pioneers – still play a major part in American life and there's no underestimating their love of 'home' – the Cornwall many only dream about. The pace was set by 79-year-old Frank Matthews, whose home in Negaunee was half buried in snow at the end of April. The pathway to his museum was completely blocked, but Frank dug his way through to show us the trophies of a lifetime spent working in and caring for the iron ore country of the Upper Peninsular. On impulse Frank said he'd follow us back home. He did just that, for his first holiday, his first trip out of his country, and an 80th birthday with long lost Cornish cousins.

The old man had an impish sense of humour. When he was asked what part Ben had played in the B.B.C. documentary 'Cornish Miner in America' he replied. "Oh, Ben didn't do all that. He painted a lot, he drove a lot, he talked to the camera when they told him, he did all the research work, pointed out some of the tricks of the States, like there are some red traffic lights that you legally have to ignore and things like the county of

Nevada, which has nothing at all to do with the State of Nevada. Then I caught him humping the equipment about a time or two, but that's about it."

In California, Grass Valley, which proudly calls itself the most Cornish of all American towns, brought Christmas forward by eight months, for Ben's benefit. Even in America, Christmas in April complete with holly wreaths, Santa Claus, pasties by the hundred and the local equivalent of pixies (the Cornish call them tommy-knockers) was enough to bring out the national television crews. Grass Valley was built on gold, dug by Cornish miners and there are still rich veins of Cornish spirit, memories that go back to Levant, Camborne and Redruth, faces and names that could take their

place in any Cornish choir, any Sunday.

Each Cornish enclave led to another, all with stories matching that of Violet Thomas, of Prestcott, in Arizona. Her grandparents were Cornish through and through, they met and married near Prestcott after long hours in a wagon train, blistered by the sun, frozen under the stars. In Arizona the first luxury was a Chinese rooming house with candles for night-time warmth. Violet Thomas, a proud American reared on Cornish traditions and steeped in Cornish atmosphere, has clear memories of her visits to Cornwall. She says, "Take me blindfolded to the Tamar Bridge and I'd still know I was in Cornwall."

MR DAVID WAY
Producer BBC TV

124

Ben Maile
WITH
'The Cornish Miners in America'
PAINTINGS AND DRAWINGS
as featured in the B.B.C. Television Documentary

Many years ago, whilst on a painting/promotional trip to the States, I found myself exploring the old cowboy town of Virginia City in Nevada up on the sombre 'Boothill', six thousand miles away from their home, and mine.

Dozens of unmistakable Cornish names challenged me from marble headstones.

Why Cornishmen among cowboys, desperados and western lawmen? All the inevitable questions demanded answers.

After years of very amateur research my findings prompted sufficient interest for the B.B.C. to send me back, yet again, with a small production crew in 1982 22,000 miles and six weeks later we returned with the material for a fascinating documentary.

This exhibition shows not only the original paintings and drawings from that trip and its cornish counterpart, but also those works that were 'left on the cutting room floor'.

THE DORCHESTER LONDON
THURSDAY, 17th MAY 1984

Nineteenth Century Cornish Mining, oil on canvas, 30" × 40"

125

Envoi

The Publisher suggests that as this is not a fictional work where normally can be appended 'The End', I should express some final thoughts. That very word 'final' is too terminal for my choice. The views that I have expressed in these pages are merely thoughts, remembrances and imaginative speculations upon places we have seen and paintings I have produced. For myself I can only hope that this last page is simply a pause between the last and the next port of call. There are still many corners of the world and of life to explore.

There are blank canvases in my studio and unfilled sketch-books. Fat tubes of paint are waiting and empty pages in my passport.

So – *Au Revoir*

Ben Maile paintings – collections

H.M. The Queen.
H.R.H. Prince Charles, Prince of Wales.
Her Grace Anne, Duchess of Westminster.
British Petroleum.
B.P. Deutscher.
Babcock International.
B.P. Alaska.
English China Clays.
The Mary Rose Trust.
Beechams Chemicals.
Wedgwood.
Triport Ferries.
Cleveland Bridge Construction Company.
P. & O. *S.S. Canberra*.
Thameside Construction Company.
N. J. Crisp Esq.
Miss Sue Lawley.
Mrs. Margaret Rule C.B.E.
Mr. Bill Owen M.B.E.
Mr. Dick Ray.
Mr. Vince Hill.
Mrs. Anne Hampson.
Mr. Tim Stoner.
Mr. John Godrich.
Mr. John Collins.
Mr. E. Coupland.
Mr. Phillip Needham.
Mr. Malcolm Cockell.
Mr. David Way.

Ben Maile paintings – a summary

GRAND CANAL VENICE

Exhibitions
Many galleries throughout the U.K. including:
The Mansion House (London).
Upper Grosvenor Gallery (London).
Medici Gallery (London).
The Whitgift Gallery (London).
Selfridges (London).
Gordon Gallery (London).
Harrods (London).
The Wedgwood Shop of Harrogate (Harrogate).
Howells Gallery (Cardiff).
Beale's Gallery (Bournemouth).
Barclay Gallery (Chester).
Imperial Gallery (Cheltenham).
Mathiesons Gallery (Edinburgh).
City Museum (Aberdeen).

Overseas
San Francisco, Paulo Alto, Reno (USA)
Toronto (Canada)
Wellington (New Zealand)
Balmoral Gallery, Geelong (Australia)
City Museum, Anchorage.

Fine Art Reproductions
Since the first in 1959 the total now comes to more than thirty.

First Signed Limited Edition
'A Time of Glory' (450) in 1974, followed by 'The Thin Red Line' (450). To date Limited Editions number fourteen; of these 'In Face of Danger' was donated to the RNLI, 'Endangered Species' to Scottish Wild Life Society and 'Mary Rose 1545' to The Mary Rose Trust.